NEW ALIGNMENTS IN AMERICAN POLITICS

edited by CARL LOWE

THE REFERENCE SHELF

Volume 52 Number 2

THE H. W. WILSON COMPANY

New York   1980

THE REFERENCE SHELF

The books in this series contain reprints of articles, excerpts from books, and addresses on current issues and social trends in the United States and other countries. There are six separately bound numbers in each volume, all of which are generally published in the same calendar year. One number is a collection of recent speeches; each of the others is devoted to a single subject and gives background information and discussion from various points of view, concluding with a comprehensive bibliography. Books in the series may be purchased individually or on subscription.

Library of Congress Cataloging in Publication Data

Main entry under title:

New alignments in American politics.

(The Reference shelf ; v. 52, no. 2)
Bibliography: p.
1. Political parties—United States—Addresses, essays, lectures.   2. Pressure groups—United States—Addresses, essays, lectures.   I.   Lowe, Carl.
II.   Series: Reference shelf ; v. 52, no. 2.
JK2261.N48   324.273   80-187
ISBN 0-8242-0645-2

PRINTED IN THE UNITED STATES OF AMERICA

CONTENTS

PREFACE

We are living through one of the most remarkable periods in our history. This bewildering struggle of advocacy groups in the United States is producing amazement elsewhere in the world. The amazement is partly admiration for the creativity of our political system and partly apprehension that we may one day tear ourselves apart in the enthusiasm of our contentiousness.

This observation by William J. McGill, president of Columbia University, in a recent speech, accurately summarizes the political situation in the United States today. Twenty years ago one could easily define the American political spectrum in terms of left, right, and center and, with the ready consensus of other political observers, place individual politicians and voting blocs within that perspective. The major parties traditionally operated as working, though sometimes shifting, coalitions of large blocs; Franklin D. Roosevelt's Democratic Party, for example, encircled within its fold allies that now find themselves uneasy political bedfellows, if not outright antagonists—organized labor, Midwestern farmers, the urban poor, Northern liberals, Solid South conservatives, blacks, ethnic and religious minorities of immigrant stock.

The validity of old political labels, however, has faded in light of the mass entry of special-interest groups that now threaten to dominate the political arena. Their arrival has been facilitated by the erosion of the traditional parties (Democratic and Republican), whose dominance of the political scene previously limited newcomers' access to political power, and by the steady growth of the mass media, which, in the vacuum left by the decline of the parties, are now voters' chief sources of information about issues and candidates.

Today, TV, radio, and newspapers provide instant access to large blocs of voters, and carefully planned media cam-

5

paigns have replaced the armies of party regulars who were
once the key tool in elections and referenda. Candidates and
groups now utilize photogenic demonstrations (televised), or
TV commercials (as well as radio and print advertisements),
which reach many more voters than pavement-pounding
doorbell ringers ever could.

Thus the rules of the American political game have
changed and these changes have strongly influenced the new
alignments taking shape today. The decline of the two major
parties and of traditional alignments has been accentuated by
political fund-raising reforms enacted by Congress in the
wake of the Watergate excesses. Whereas a party was once a
candidate's main source of money and campaign workers,
funds and organization now derive from outside sources. The
administrative structures created by Congress to oversee expenditures funnel money to individual candidates and not to
parties. This situation, some have suggested, threatens to reduce the parties to being just another special-interest group,
standing on the outside of the political process looking in. An
external threat such as the prolonged imprisonment of
American hostages by a hostile government in Iran may forge
a very broad new alignment—the entire nation, unified in one
cause, across and within party lines. Once the foreign threat
diminishes, however, the narrow conflicts resume.

This compilation explores the current political situation,
the changes in alignments that have taken place, and their
ramifications, as well as changes that are likely to take place
in the near future. Section I is an overview, tracing the roots
of the American party system, exploring how the alignments
that are now undergoing convulsive change were born. Section II examines conflicting political philosophies that are
vying for the minds and hearts of voters, philosophies advo-
cated by those who dream of creating new parties to challenge the power of the old ones. Section III looks at activist
movements—special-interest groups that rally around issues
and, in their single-mindedness, eschew coalition politics.

Section IV focuses on forces that will strongly influence the future. These include new fund-raising techniques as well as the evolving structure of campaigns.

The compiler wishes to thank the authors and publishers who have courteously granted permission for the reprinting of their materials.

CARL LOWE

December 1979

I. THE MAJOR PARTIES: FLOURISHING OR IN DECLINE?

EDITOR'S INTRODUCTION

In the opinion of many informed observers, both of the major parties have seen their power decline on the national political scene. This decline is reflected in the attitudes of voters and elected officials. Each year, more and more voters register as independents, instead of aligning themselves with the Republicans or the Democrats, and many are proud to boast that they vote for the man or woman who is running for office and not for the party. As a result, those elected to the Senate and House of Representatives feel less loyalty to their party because of the diminished importance of party support in their successful campaign strategies.

In the first excerpt in this section, James Q. Wilson, a professor of government at Harvard writing in *Commentary*, notes that the "atomization" of political institutions leads elected officials to resist efforts to have them vote the party line. The lack of party discipline lessens party impact on legislation and increases the importance of ideology and ideas.

Everett Carll Ladd, Jr., director of the Roper Center at the University of Connecticut, writing in *Fortune*, sees large problems ahead for the two major parties in the wake of current political developments: "Democrats and Republicans alike face grave difficulties as they try to make some coherent aggregate out of the new cultural issues in order to build majority coalitions. Because these issues turn on pivotal social values, they stubbornly resist traditional formulas or stratagems for political compromise."

Pulitzer prizewinning historian Arthur Schlesinger, a professor at the City University of New York, bemoans in a *Wall Street Journal* article the effects of "electronic manipulators"—television and computers—on the traditional party

9

system and warns of the dangers of new alignments of political power "concentrated in political adventurers, in the interest groups that finance them and in the executive bureaucracy."

Agreeing with Schlesinger's view is G. M. Pomper, chairman of the department of political science at Rutgers, who in an essay reprinted from *Political Science Quarterly* cautions that the decline in the parties will make most members of society politically powerless and produce in government a "fundamental conservatism," there being "no alternate agency available to generate the political power of a popular majority."

Lance Morrow, a writer for *Time,* points out in the next article that the degeneration of the parties, which is probably a reversible phenomenon, makes practically every politician a free agent and can lead to a proliferation of "single-issue zealotry."

Alan Baron, Washington editor of *Politics Today,* finds a new spirit of pragmatism in the Republican Party that may prove to be its salvation. If it can overcome the ideological conflicts that have divided it and diluted its strength, a development most other observers deem unlikely, Baron sees the GOP's resurgence as a powerful national party.

Also writing in *Politics Today,* William Schneider discovers a "gradual rationalization of Southern politics." In his view, Southern voters are freeing themselves from their obsession with segregation politics and aligning with Democrats or Republicans according to economic interests.

The next article, a September 1978 *U.S. News & World Report* survey, points up the growing role minorities and women have taken in the two major parties. By accommodating such traditionally apolitical or alienated sectors of the electorate, the article concludes, the major parties may find new sources of political clout in the future and, perhaps, regain the strength they have lost. The same weekly, however, surveying the political scene one year later, presents a more clouded picture. The updated look—a forecast for the 1980s—places the blame for the decline of political parties on "efforts to open them up to broader public participation," efforts that have supplanted the power of experienced politicians and created weak parties led by ineffective newcomers.

AMERICAN POLITICS, THEN & NOW[1]

The administration of President Carter offers an appropriate occasion for asking a question that will be raised with growing frequency as this nation approaches the bicentennial observance of the writing of the Constitution: has the American political system changed fundamentally? If no accident befalls him, Jimmy Carter will be the first Democrat in this century to serve a full term in the White House without having to lead the nation into war or out of economic disaster. Indeed, the historical rarity of the present moment is even more striking: Carter is (so far) the first Democratic President since before the Civil War to serve a full term without either war or depression and to have a Democratic majority in both houses of Congress. The Carter administration offers, in this sense, an example of a "normal" administration in the hands of what has become the nation's dominant political party.

Would the political system inherited by President Carter be recognized by its architect, James Madison? Or by the powerful Republican Senators of the late 19th century? Or even by Harry Truman? We can turn to the *Federalist Papers* for an account of what that system was supposed to be in 1787; if that seems too antiquarian a source for the restlessly contemporary modern mind, we can turn to descriptions written a generation ago by leading journalists and political scientists.

In 1948, the late John Fischer published in *Harper's* magazine an article on the "Unwritten Rules of American Politics"

[1] Excerpted from magazine article by James Q. Wilson, Shattuck Professor of Government, Harvard University. *Commentary.* 67:39–46. F. '79. Reprinted from *Commentary*, February 1979, by permission; all rights reserved.

that was at the time, and for many years thereafter, widely recognized as the best brief analysis of the distinctive features of American politics. He drew upon the writings of John C. Calhoun, the South Carolina politician and intellectual who nearly a century before had set forth the doctrine of the "concurrent majority." In Calhoun's time, of course, that doctrine was a defense of the Southern resistance to federal legislation aimed at restricting the spread of slavery, but Fischer, aided by the writings of Peter Drucker, found in the theory of the concurrent majority, stripped of its extremist and partisan language, an enduring and fundamental explanation of the American constitutional system.

That system was designed to preserve liberty and maintain a national union by a set of procedures meant to insure that no important decision would be reached without the concurrence of each interest vitally affected by that decision. In Congress, no important bloc would be voted down on any matter that touched its central concern. In nominating a presidential candidate, no one would be acceptable who was objectionable to any significant body of opinion within the party. In electing a President, both parties would sacrifice any interest in principle or policy to accommodate the views of the average voter and thus would almost always offer an echo, not a choice. Politics would be non-ideological, conflict would be minimized, and such policies as survived the process of interest-group bargaining would command widespread support and thus be likely to endure. . . .

Persons who believe that all this has changed point to the legislative explosion that occurred during the 1960's and early 1970's. Without benefit of a national emergency which in the past had always been necessary for the system of veto groups to be set aside, there poured forth from Congress an unprecedented wave of policy innovation. The Southern filibuster was broken and civil-rights bills became law. The caution of the House Ways and Means Committee was overcome and Medicare and Medicaid were passed. The fears of federal control of schools that for long prevented federal aid to education were set aside and such aid became a massive and growing reality. The War on Poverty, the model-cities program, and the rest of the Great Society legislation arrived, to be followed, toward the end of the 1960's, by the emergence of environmental and consumer legislation. Between 1966 and 1970, at least eighteen major consumer-protection laws and seven major air- and water-pollution laws were passed, and the activity continued well into the 1970's. . . .

II

The opposite view is that, despite the frenzy of the 1960's, nothing of fundamental importance changed. The Carter Presidency has been functioning rather much like the Truman Presidency: unheroically, with little public enthusiasm, winning some battles and losing others. Liberal ideas of 1948, such as civil rights, national health insurance, and federal aid to education, were defeated; liberal ideas of 1976, such as national health insurance, welfare and tax revisions, and new labor laws, were likewise defeated. Though the nation was at peace in 1948 as in 1976, both Presidents were preoccupied in large measure with foreign affairs—the Marshall Plan, NATO, and international trade in the case of Truman; the Panama Canal, tension in the Middle East, and relations with Turkey in the case of Carter. Both Presidents saw Congress debate at length a bill to deregulate natural gas and neither President was able to get out of the debate exactly what he wanted. Truman vetoed a deregulation bill passed in 1950, Carter signed a compromise deregulation bill in 1978. During his first year in office, Carter won on 75 per cent of the congressional votes taken on his program, far lower than the level of support enjoyed by Eisenhower, Kennedy, or Johnson in their first or second years. . . .

III

Both interpretations of American politics are partially correct. Congress remains able, long after the 1960's, to pass sweeping new laws almost without regard to the normal constraints of interest-group bargaining, as it did when it decided in 1978 to abolish mandatory retirement before age seventy or decided in 1973 to give absolute protection to endangered species. And Congress continues to experience great difficulty in formulating a coherent policy on matters such as taxation, energy, or school desegregation. As Anthony King has recently observed, our political system has acquired the contradictory tendencies of a human crowd—"to move either very sluggishly or with extreme speed." (*The New American Political System*, 1978, p 393)

Three things account for the schizophrenia of contemporary politics: one is the greater ease with which decisions can be transferred from the private to the public sphere; a second is the "atomization," as King terms it, of political institutions; a third is a change in the governing ideas of our time. The first factor has caused the American law-making system to be in a state of permanent excitability; the second has made the outcome of any excitement difficult to predict; and the third has been the source of the energy that determines whether the system will be in its manic or depressive phase.

Madison and the other framers of the Constitution created, as everyone knows, a federal government designed to prevent the mischief of faction and the tyranny of temporary majorities by so arranging its institutions that ambition would be made to check ambition. Douglass C. North, the economic historian, has stated one consequence of the Madisonian system this way: in order to reduce the ability of interest groups to capture the government, the constitutional order attached a high cost to utilizing the political system as compared to the marketplace for making decisions. The "entry price" for politics was high, and thus only the largest or most popular factions were able to pay it. This price was both tangible and intangible. The material cost was the great effort required to organize groups (parties, factions, lobbies) influential enough to get an issue onto the agenda of Congress and to coordinate the decision of Congress (and its many parts) and the President. The non-material cost was the widespread belief that a large range of issues—public welfare, civil rights, the regulation of economic enterprise, even for a while the building of public works—was outside the legitimate scope of federal authority.

The late E. E. Schattschneider once observed that "he who decides what politics is about runs the country." Once politics was about only a few things; today, it is about nearly everything. There has been, in North's terms, a "drastic reduction in the cost of using the political process" relative to the cost of using, for similar results, the market. That reduction has been the result of easier access to the courts (by fee-shifting and class-action suits), the greater ease of financing interest groups with foundation grants and direct-mail fundraising, and the multiplication of government agencies and congressional staffs.

Not only have the money costs of using political strategies fallen, the ideological costs have declined as well. Until rather recently, the chief issue in any congressional argument over new policies was whether it was legitimate for the federal government to do something at all. That was the crux of the dispute over Social Security, welfare, Medicare, civil rights, selective service, foreign aid, international alliances, price and wage controls, economic regulation, and countless other departures from the past. But once the initial law is passed, the issue of legitimacy disappears, and, except in those few cases where the Supreme Court later holds the law unconstitutional, does not reemerge.

Once the "legitimacy barrier" has fallen, political conflict takes a very different form. New programs need not await the advent of a crisis or an extraordinary majority, because no program is any longer "new"—it is seen, rather, as an extension, a modification, or an enlargement of something the government is already doing. Congressmen will argue about "how much," or "where," or "what kind," but not about "whether." One consequence is that the workload of Congress will grow astronomically.

Since there is virtually nothing the government has not tried to do, there is little it cannot be asked to do. Congressmen try frantically to keep up with this growing workload by adding to their staffs, but of course a bigger staff does not produce less work, it produces more, and so the ideas, demands, and commitments presented daily to a legislator grow even faster. Moreover, Congress creates a bureaucracy of its own to keep up with the information-gathering and policy-generating capacities of the executive branch, leading to what Senator Daniel P. Moynihan has characterized as the "Iron Law of Emulation." (*Commentary*, June 1978)

This dramatic expansion of the political agenda has helped alter the distribution of political power. At one time, the legislative process was biased in favor of the opponents of any new policy. The committee system and the great powers of committee chairmen meant that the crucial calculation to be made by a proponent of a new policy was not how many congressmen were in favor of it, but which congressmen were opposed to it. The fact that the proposed policy was new and that there were few or no precedents for governmental action in that area made it easier for a Wilbur Mills, a James Eastland, or a Howard Smith to use their position on the House Ways and Means Committee, the Senate Judiciary Committee, or the House Rules Committee to block consideration of the proposal. But when the government is already doing something in the area, then there is an existing agency of government, and its asociated private supporters with a stake in the matter, and at the very least the appropriations bill for that agency, and usually the legislative amendments proposed by that agency, must be considered.

Political scientists have frequently described American policy-making as "incremental." Some have used the term admiringly, because the process it describes builds consensus; others have used it critically, because that process prevents radical change and misrepresents some interests. But whatever one thinks of the concept, it is increasingly hard to believe it generally descriptive. We have brought under new regulatory machinery whole sectors of our economy; changed in one sudden blow the legality of a mandatory retirement age; rewritten (in a manner almost no one understands) the basic law governing retirement systems; banned the use of

whole categories of chemicals; given to Congress a legislative
veto over important parts of our foreign policy once reserved
entirely for the President; adopted a vast and expensive system for financing health care; put under public auspices a
large part of the American rail system; created public financing of presidential campaigns; changed the meaning of
"equality of opportunity" from "fair competition" to "the
achievement of racial goals"; and come close to authorizing
cash grants to parents of children attending parochial schools
and private colleges. These may be good ideas or they may be
bad ones, but it is hard to describe them—and dozens of
others like them—as "marginal" or "incremental" changes in
policy.

IV

The second change has been the atomization of certain
key political institutions, notably Congress and the political
parties. Congress has, to a degree, been de-institutionalized
and individualized: its leadership has become weaker, power
within it has been dispersed, the autonomy and resources of
its individual members have been enlarged. As a result, it is
no longer helpful to think of Congress as consisting of blocs,
each representing an interest group and each having a potential veto over measures affecting its vital interests. This might
strike some readers as a gain—vested interests can no longer
so easily say no to things they oppose. But such a view ne-
glects the price that has been paid for this: if nobody can say
no and make it stick, then neither can anybody say yes and
make it stick. If there are no vetoes, neither are there any
imprimaturs.

The individual member of Congress has gained enormously at the expense of committee chairmen, party leaders,
and interest groups. He or she now has a large personal staff
and a voice in the choice of the staff members of committees.
(The congressional bureaucracy is probably the fastest-grow-
ing one in Washington, with no nonsense about civil service
to inhibit it. The staff in 1976 was three times larger than it

was in 1956.) The seniority system no longer governs the
choice of committee chairmen to the exclusion of all other
considerations; in 1975, House Democrats, by secret ballot,
deposed three committee chairmen and elevated in their
stead more junior members. Committees no longer regularly
meet behind closed doors (whereas almost half of all House
committee meetings were closed to the public in 1972, only 3
per cent were by 1975). Al Ullman cannot dominate the Ways
and Means Committee the way Wilbur Mills once did, it is
unlikely that Robert Byrd or his successors will have the
power that Lyndon Johnson did when he was Senate majority
leader, and though Tip O'Neill is a stronger Speaker than
Carl Albert, he is a far cry from Sam Rayburn.

Some of the enhanced autonomy and status of individual,
especially junior, members of Congress was won by backbench revolts against leadership, but much of it was given to
them by leaders attempting to build their own power by
doing lasting favors for the rank-and-file. When Lyndon
Johnson was Senate majority leader, his stature among fresh-
men Senators was high in part because he adopted a practice
in the 1950's of giving to each new Senator at least one major
committee assignment rather than, as had once been the case,
of making them wait patiently for the "Club" to admit them
into the ranks of the deserving. Among the latter-day beneficiaries of this generosity were George McGovern and Walter
Mondale. In 1970, with only six years' seniority, McGovern
became chairman of a Select Committee on Hunger and
Mondale, with only seven years of service, chairman of a
Committee on School Segregation. The well-publicized hearings of these committees did not harm the political ambitions
of their youthful chairmen. In decentralizing power in Congress in order to enhance (temporarily) the power of a given
leader, the leader is acting much like the man who keeps his
house warm in the winter by burning in his fireplace the fur-
niture, the doors, and the walls. Soon there is nothing left to
burn.

It is not just the formal apparatus of party and leadership
in Congress that is weaker, but the informal and social organi-

zation as well. Not long after Fischer wrote, William White described the Senate "Club" of veteran, chiefly Southern, Senators who dominated its affairs and acted, not surprisingly, entirely in the spirit of Calhoun and the concurrent majority. Within a decade after White wrote, the "Club" was pretty much finished, the victim of deaths, retirements, defeats, and—above all—political change. In 1949, in the Congress elected when Fischer was writing, Southerners held twice as many committee chairmanships as did Northerners and Westerners combined. By 1977, the Southern committee chairman was the exception, not the rule. In the period 1947–56, Gary Orfield notes, half of *all* the Democrats in Congress were from the South; today, less than one-third are.

Individual members of Congress are far more secure in their seats than once was the case, and with increased security goes increased freedom from those organizations, be they political parties or interest groups, that once controlled the resources necessary for reelection. Between 1952 and 1974, only about 6 percent of the incumbent representatives seeking reelection were defeated, a substantial decline from earlier in this century. Moreover, of those running for reelection, fewer face close contests. When Fischer wrote in 1948, the winner of most House contests received 55 per cent of the vote or less. By 1972, most winners received 60 per cent of the vote or more. As political scientists like David Mayhew have pointed out, safe seats have become the rule, not the exception. Barring major electoral turnovers, such as in 1964, it may be that most new entrants to Congress will come from those districts where incumbents have decided voluntarily to retire.

Campaign-finance laws will strengthen this pattern. By restricting individual donations to $1,000, they limit sharply the chances of unknown and unwealthy candidates amassing large war chests to challenge well-known incumbents. By restricting donations from special-interests groups to $5,000, they limit the extent to which money can be the basis of group influence over legislators. (Rich candidates can still finance their own campaigns without restriction.) And if public

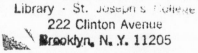

financing of congressional campaigns should become law, one
can be confident Congress will see to it that this "reform,"
like all others it has enacted, serves the advantage of incumbents.

The individualization and decentralization of Congress
that has been the result of these changes in its internal affairs
has been further augmented by the general decline of the political party, the increased use of radio and television for
building personal followings in election campaigns, and the
emergence of campaign organizations, often designed and
staffed by professional campaign consultants, that are the
personal property of the candidate rather than the collective
effort of the party.

One consequence of these changes can be seen most dramatically in the Senate. From 1900 to 1956, only 30 per cent
of the major-party candidates for President or Vice President
came from the United States Senate; between 1960 and 1976,
70 per cent were Senators. The Senate has become the incu-
bator of Presidents. When parties cannot pick presidential
candidates but instead meet in conventions to ratify the
choices made in two dozen or more primary elections and
hundreds of local community caucuses, they discover they are
often choosing among Senators because of the enormous advantage these persons have in developing a national reputation. The Senate is covered by the national press in a way the
House is not; skillful and ambitious Senators can preside over
dramatic hearings (into auto safety, the drug industry, malnu-
trition, organized crime, or intelligence-gathering) that are
televised. Senators have the resources (a Senator from New
York, for example, has a staff budget of around $1 million a
year) to develop issues and reach national constituencies with
which they wish to be identified. Computers can be pro-
grammed to produce huge and precisely indexed national
mailing lists useful for reaching both voters and contributors.

When Fischer wrote, presidential candidates were still
picked by conventions in which party "bosses" were influential. In 1948 there were presidential primaries in only fourteen states, and in five of these unpledged delegations ran at

large. The open party caucus was almost unheard of. Though the Democratic party was deeply split among its ideological factions, the extremists of the Left and the Right did not contest the primaries but organized instead as independent parties. President Truman had only nominal opposition at the 1948 convention. In 1976, there were primaries in over two dozen states, wide open local caucuses in many others, and President Ford faced serious opposition in both the primaries and the convention. In each party, the ideological divisions were obvious and wide. Party regularity was an important consideration in 1948 for convention delegate and presidential candidate alike; anybody who used such a term in 1976 would have elicited either a smile or a yawn. When compromises were made in 1948, they were made to attract the middle-of-the-road voter; when they were made in 1976, it was to appease the more militant party activists (Walter Mondale was put on the Carter ticket to soothe the liberals, Robert Dole put on the Ford ticket to help please the conservatives). That Carter, a governor with no clear record on national issues, was able to win the Democratic nomination, was right in keeping with the political style of 1948; in 1976, however, it was seen as a curiosity to be explained by the temporary triumph of image over ideology in the wake of Watergate.

All these factors have tended to make the Congress of today, in comparison with that about which Fischer wrote in 1948, a collection of individuals rather than blocs. More precisely, blocs exist, but they are typically formed by the Congressmen themselves, on the basis of personal political convictions or broad allegiances to regions or sectors of society, rather than in response to, or as an instrument of, an organized interest outside Congress. Perhaps the largest and most significant bloc today is the Democratic Study Group, an organization of liberal Democrats in the House. It has leaders, a staff, a budget, regular meetings; its influence is hard to measure, but far from trivial. There is also a Black Caucus and a Northeast-Midwest Economic Advancement Coalition. In 1948, Congressmen were more likely to organize into a "farm bloc," or a "labor bloc," or an "oil bloc." Such

influences still operate, of course, but groups based on ideology or racial or ethnic identification have become more important than those based on economic interest. And
Congressmen change their minds more frequently, making it
harder to count in advance on their position.

More assertive and individualistic members combined
with fewer sources of influence mean that more effort must be
devoted to rounding up votes. In the House, Representative
John Brademas, the Democratic whip, is assisted by no fewer
than 35 deputy or assistant whips and spends on this vote-
producing operation over $400,000 a year, more than three
times as much as was spent in 1970. One assistant whip with
long experience recently complained that his job is "a hell of
a lot more difficult than it used to be."

The individualization of politics has meant that interest
groups have had to individualize their appeal and link it
directly to the electoral fortunes of individual Congressmen.
Thus, the rise of "grass-roots" lobbying—the careful, often
computerized mobilization of letters, mailgrams, delegations,
and financial contributions from individual citizens in each
legislator's district or state. When the AFL-CIO was locked
in struggle with the business-oriented National Action Committee on Labor Law Reform, the two sides were estimated to
have generated nearly five million pieces of mail to Congress.
Mark Green, director of Ralph Nader's Congress Watch, said
that grass-roots lobbying has made Washington "an absolutely different city these days." Today, he noted, "you lose
bills in the districts, not in Washington."

V

But if key political institutions are becoming so atomized,
how does any policy get passed? The explanation, I suspect, is
to be found in the third change in politics—the enhanced importance of ideas and of ideology. To return to Anthony
King's metaphor, what makes the difference between the
sluggish and the rushing crowd is the force of a compelling
idea.

The Congress of 1968 or 1978, much more than that of 1948, is susceptible to the power of ideas whenever there seems to be a strong consensus as to what the correct ideas are. Such a consensus existed in the mid-1960's about the Great Society legislation; no such consensus about these matters exists today. This helps explain, as Henry J. Aaron has noted, the changing prospects of social-welfare policies. Consumerism, ecology, campaign-finance reform, and congressional ethics are other examples of ideas with strong symbolic appeal that, so long as the consensus endures, are handled by a political process in which the advantage lies with the proponents of change.

When a consensus evaporates or a symbol loses its power, issues are handled by a process which, like that in 1948, gives the advantage to the opponents of change. But sooner or later, a scandal, a shift in the focus of media attention, or the efforts of a skilled policy entrepreneur such as Ralph Nader or John Gardner will bring a compelling new idea to the top of the political agenda, and once again action will become imperative.

I do not wish to enter the argument whether there has been an "end of ideology" in the West or whether there is a heightened degree of "ideological constraint" in the public at large. Within Congress, however, the Republican party seems to have become more consistently conservative and the Democratic party more consistently liberal. Whatever has happened in society, the principle of affiliation among legislators has become, I think, more clearly based on shared ideas, and to a degree those shared ideas conform to party labels. (More accurately, the notion of party in Congress has been infused with more ideological meaning by its members.)

The point is debatable and easily overstated, but one illustration suggests what may have happened. In 1949, the House voted on a bill to deregulate natural gas. The influence of party was scarcely detectable and, had we the data, the influence of ideology only slightly more so. The Democrats split almost evenly (49 per cent in favor, 51 per cent opposed); the Republicans were a bit more lopsided (73 per cent in favor,

24   The Reference Shelf

27 per cent opposed). In 1977, the House voted again on a comparable though not identical bill. Now, the influence of party was almost complete: 75 per cent of the Democrats opposed it; 88 per cent of the Republicans favored it. Pietro Novola at the University of Vermont has found that ideology and partisanship were vastly more important than economic interest (whether one comes from a gas-consuming or gas-producing district) in explaining the 1977 congressional vote.

Much attention has rightly been paid to one source of politically influential ideas—the "New Class" composed of persons having high levels of education and professional occupations. This group is decidedly more liberal than other groups in society, so much so that Everett Ladd was able to conclude that by the early 1960's, a majority of the "privileged" elements in society considered themselves Democrats and voted for Democratic candidates for Congress. The New Class is responsive to, and provides support for, politicians who favor abortion on demand, environmental- and consumer-protection laws, and equal rights for women. [For an article by Everett Ladd on the new divisions in American politics, see the selection that follows.—Ed.]

But every class has its counterpart class. The discussion of the New Class, and even its label, leads attention away from what is happening to other, non-liberal groups in society. Upper-middle-class white Northern Protestants, once the bastion of traditional conservatism, have not been converted into a liberal New Class, they have been split into two deeply opposed groups. Sidney Verba and his co-workers found that in the 1950's, this group was the most conservative identifiable segment of American opinion. By the 1970's, however, a profound change had occurred—one part of this group had become even more conservative, while another part had become very liberal. High-status Wasps are now the most polarized class in America, and to the extent that this class contributes disproportionately to political elites, these elites have become more polarized.

These divisions of opinion contribute powerfully to the kind of "one-issue" politics so characteristic of the present

era. Pro-abortion versus pro-life; gun control versus the right
to bear arms; gay rights versus traditional values; ERA versus
anti-ERA; nuclear energy versus solar energy; proponents of
affirmative action versus opponents of reverse discrimination—all these causes and more make life miserable for the
traditional, coalition-seeking politician. Weakened institutions, individualized politics, and the rise of an educated,
idea-oriented public combine to make it highly advantageous
for political entrepreneurs to identify and mobilize single-
issue constituencies and to enlist them, not only into electoral
and legislative politics, but into court suits, referendum campaigns, and even calls for constitutional conventions.

The importance of single-issue politics is, of course, much
discussed, but not without a touch of hypocrisy. Most columnists and commentators began to criticize this phenomenon
only when it took directions of which they did not approve.
Anti-war politics, the drive for abortion on demand, the effort
to obtain gun control, and the opposition to nuclear energy
are typically described by liberals as "movements" or "concerns." When the right-to-life forces or those opposing gun
control get organized, however, their critics not only disap-
prove of their ideas, they deplore their use of "extremist"
tactics.

To the extent that ideas determine whether the atomized
political system will move speedily, sluggishly, or not at all,
the principal task of political analysis becomes that of understanding the processes whereby certain ideas become dominant. This requires more subtle techniques for studying
public opinion than any that have been routinely employed,
techniques that will measure the intensity of feeling as well as
its distribution and will distinguish opinions capable of providing the basis for political mobilization from those that are
mere expressions of preference. And we require better knowledge about the organizations that shape opinion—the mass
and elite media, the universities, and those acronymic groups
that manage to devise and implant compelling slogans.

In John Fischer's day, scholars studied big business, labor
unions, medical societies, and farm groups. Today, we need to

understand better how elites learn ideas in their colleges and
law schools and from the magazines of opinion. How else can
we explain, for example, why a generation of legislators who
believed in the virtues of business regulation by independent
commissions is being replaced by one seeking to deregulate
many of those businesses, often over the bitter objections of
the regulated industry? Or why a generation that applauded
John F. Kennedy's inaugural promise to defend liberty anywhere, at any price, has become one that prefers to minimize
risks of every kind, in every place?

VI

We are at a loss for a word or phrase to describe the new
features of the political system; scholars even disagree as to
whether it is all that new. Such terms as "veto-group politics"
seemed most appropriate for the system that Fischer and
later David Riesman described thirty years ago; that powerful
insight allowed many discrete facts to be summarized in one
economical statement. Today, the system is more confused
and so our political vocabulary has become more prolix and
less precise.

Viewed in a longer historical perspective, what we are
seeing may not be all that new. The Congress in which Madison and his immediate successors sat was highly individualized. Strong, institutionalized congressional leadership did
not emerge until the latter half of the 19th century; one contest for Speaker in 1856 ran to 133 ballots. Factions
abounded, but national interest-group organization did not
occur until the end of the 19th century. "Single-issue" politics
existed, the abolition of slavery being the most conspicuous
example. But in Madison's time, and for many decades thereafter, national politics was less a career than a hobby; the federal government played a minor role in human affairs; the
range of issues with which Congress had to deal was small;
and ideological cleavages tended to occur one at a time. Now,
governing is a profession, the government plays a large role,
and issues tend to pile up, one atop the other, in a network of

multiple and profound ideological cleavages. Whether one describes as "fundamental" the changes in institutions and ideas that have accompanied the rise of modern government is in part a matter of style. Yet one must be impressed by the change in the dominant ethos of the times—whereas the period 1890–1920 was the great era of institution-building in voluntary associations, political parties, corporate enterprises, and congressional leadership, the last decade or so has been one that has criticized, attacked, and partially dismantled institutions.

From a broader, international perspective, one might say that the changes I have described add up to nothing of fundamental importance. The American constitutional order, with its separate executive and legislative branches and its independent judiciary, remains very different from the British system of cabinet-in-parliament. And so it does. (It is ironic to note the stirrings among British politicians who would like to see their system, which stifles the backbench member of Commons, changed into something more "American." They may suppose that they can combine the advantages of strong party government with the advantages of powerful legislative committees and more autonomous legislators, but I suspect they are wrong.)

By the standards of liberals and socialists, the American system remains far more conservative than that of European democracies. Where is our national health insurance, our comprehensive income-maintenance scheme, our government ownership of key industries? By these tests, the American system *is* conservative. But by another test it is far more activist and innovative than almost any European democracy: what other country has anything like our detailed federal regulation of business enterprise, our elaborate set of "tax expenditures," our affirmative-action programs addressed to the demands of a growing list of ethnic and racial minorities? Some rather careful distinctions must be made before one can compare how American policy-making differs from that abroad.

What is more striking to me is that, since the 1930's, there has occurred in this country an extraordinary redistribution of political power without any prior redistribution of income or wealth. Those persons, of the Right as well as the Left, who are enchanted with economic explanations of political life have their work cut out for them if they insist on ignoring the powerful transformation in *ideas* that seems to lie at the heart of these changes.

THE NEW DIVISIONS IN
U.S. POLITICS[2]

Over the past several years, the last strongly distinctive features of the class and policy cleavages dating from the New Deal era have finally been swept away. This transformation of political conflict began in the 1960's, and it progressed in stages. But the break from the past has now become sharp and unmistakable. And both new commitments and new divisions appear almost certain to prevail at least throughout the decade ahead, creating a new setting in which political parties compete and policy decisions get made.

Unfortunately, the understanding of these changes in political ideology tends to be clouded by the long-standing American penchant for obfuscating terminology. *Nomen est numen*, the old maxim goes: "To name is to know." There is, of course, a corollary: *Falsum nomen est confusio.* In the New Deal years, the principal political divisions came to be described in terms of liberalism and conservatism. Today there persists the habit of trying to describe candidates, contending groups, and policy preferences with the same old labels. When this palpably does not work—and labels and realities are at obvious odds—we take refuge in prefixes. Thus our po-

[2] Reprint of magazine article by Everett Carll Ladd, Jr., author and executive director of the Roper Center, University of Connecticut, assisted by Dana Suszkiw, a research associate of the Roper Center. *Fortune.* 99:88–92+. Mr. 26, '79. Reprinted from the March 26 issue of FORTUNE Magazine by special permission. © 1979 Time Inc.

litical vocabulary has become replete with categories like new liberalism, neoconservatism, new right, and old left. But none of these terms really acknowledges that present-day conflicts differ fundamentally—both in policy substance and in the way social groups are aligned—from the splits of the preceding decades.

If our vocabulary for the current ideological cleavages seems antiquated and confused, however, the realities are not obscure at all. Two major developments have been radically remaking the political landscape:

First, the big economic issues—such matters as the appropriate role for government in economic life, business versus labor, taxation, and spending for social programs—no longer reflect any coherent class divisions. It was very different twenty and thirty years ago, when lower socioeconomic groups espoused a liberal political economy—specifically, a big new interventionist role for government—while the preponderance of the middle classes held to a conservative approach. All manner of groups still pursue their special economic interests, of course. But there is nothing so overarching and persistent as the great working-class/middle-class split of the New Deal era.

This virtual end to class conflict in the economic sphere has been accompanied by widespread agreement on two basic propositions: (1) that there is no alternative to a major role by government in regulating the economy, providing social services, and assuring economic progress; and (2) that inflation is the fundamental economic problem, and government—with its escalating spending and deficits—bears prime responsibility for it. This combination of judgments is neither "liberal" nor "conservative," and any such description can only confuse and mislead.

Second, as the familiar economic divisions have vanished, a new form of class conflict has evolved from the pace of *social* and *cultural* change. In the 1960's and 1970's, the provocative and divisive questions had to do with such issues as civil rights, the position of women, the status of the family, sexual conduct, use of drugs, attitudes toward work, and moral mat-

ters like abortion. In each of these areas, support for change
has not been distributed evenly across the population, but
rather has been decisively shaped by social background. The
resulting divisions have been determined less by a citizen's
class in the traditional sense—his occupation and the amount
of his income—than by his exposure to contrasting cultural
milieus.

Considered in these terms, the distance from the 1930's is
vast. It is true that the differences between upper-income and
lower-income Americans during New Deal years was often
overstated, and the country was far from class warfare. But
the events of the time brought economic issues to a sharp
focus, and made for a split between business and labor more
distinct than ever before in the U.S.

The polls of that time make this clear. The nationalization
of business firms was seriously argued, and the issue split the
population rather clearly on class lines. As the chart on page
32 indicates, some two-thirds of unskilled workers in 1937 favored government ownership of the banks—as against less
than one-third of those in business and professional jobs. A
majority of low-income Americans favored limits on the size
of private fortunes, whereas large majorities of the upper-income groups opposed any such limits. The trend toward more
government regulation of business, supported by the working
class, was strongly opposed by the middle class. Three-quarters of unskilled workers—but less than half of professionals
and managers—maintained that business profits were too big.

The reason for such a consistent pattern of divisions is not
hard to uncover. Liberalism and conservatism spoke to contrasting interests and perceptions of society's "haves" and
"have-nots," as they were commonly called. An effort was
under way to change the balance of power in this society—an
effort that required the government to get into the act on
labor's side. Liberalism meant accelerating this effort. Conservatism meant resisting any such designs.

At this same time, however, the division over issues outside the economic realm followed little consistent pattern.
Higher-status Americans in the 1930's were more interna-

tionally minded than the working class. But on most of the
social issues of the 1930's, class differences were modest indeed. If anything, the upper-status groups were a bit more
conservative on these matters. For example, the death pen-
alty for convicted murderers was backed in 1936 by 69 percent of businessmen and professionals and by 63 percent of
unskilled and semiskilled workers. In short, the liberal-conservative division was located strictly in the arena of economic policy throughout the Depression decade.

Over the 1940's, 1950's, and 1960's, even though new economic controversies arose and old ones faded, the New Deal
pattern generally held. At the end of the 1970's, however, the
familiar class divisions are nowhere to be found. The current
campaigns to restrict the growth of government—as through
measures stipulating balanced budgets or limiting public
spending—are supported alike by the most privileged segments of society and by the most economically disadvantaged. A few months ago, 87 percent of manual workers told
Gallup interviewers that they favored a constitutional
amendment mandating a balanced federal budget—a proportion actually higher by twelve percentage points than the
support for such an amendment among business and professional people. And backing for big tax cuts, à la Proposition
13, reaches almost identical proportions among all occupa-
tional and income groups.

Gone, too, are the old perceptions of business and labor as
natural foes. The percentage of Americans in the highest income positions holding favorable views of union leaders, for
example, matches exactly with the lowest income group.
Identical proportions of those earning $25,000 a year or
more—and those from families with annual incomes of $7,000
or less— profess favorable opinions of business corporations.
On the question of whether big business is likely to pose a
threat to American society over the next two or three decades, it is high-income citizens who—completely reversing
the historical pattern—are actually more troubled by large-
business enterprise than are blue-collar workers.

Many of the new economic issues that have emerged—

THE SHARP CLASS CONFLICTS OF THE 1930's

During the New Deal years, an array of economic issues deeply and consistently divided the electorate along lines of occupation and income. This chart shows the constant pattern: the higher a citizen's class, the surer his opposition to liberal policies. By the late 1970's, however, this pattern has been erased (as seen in the facing chart). Instead, there appears a striking uniformity in political opinions of both higher-income and lower-income groups—and a disappearance of the traditional liberal-conservative split.

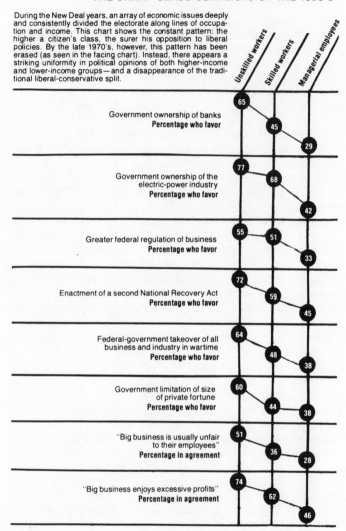

	Unskilled workers	Skilled workers	Managerial employees
Government ownership of banks Percentage who favor	65	45	29
Government ownership of the electric-power industry Percentage who favor	77	68	42
Greater federal regulation of business Percentage who favor	55	51	33
Enactment of a second National Recovery Act Percentage who favor	72	59	45
Federal-government takeover of all business and industry in wartime Percentage who favor	64	48	38
Government limitation of size of private fortune Percentage who favor	60	44	38
"Big business is usually unfair to their employees" Percentage in agreement	51	36	28
"Big business enjoys excessive profits" Percentage in agreement	74	62	46

SOURCE: Combined 1936-37 American Institute of Public Opinion (Gallup) surveys.

THE BLURRED DIVISIONS OF THE 1970's

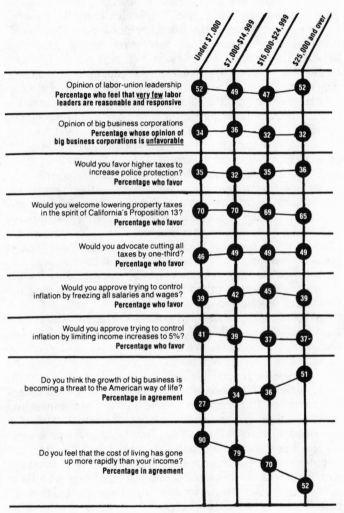

	Under $7,000	$7,000-$14,999	$15,000-$24,999	$25,000 and over
Opinion of labor-union leadership Percentage who feel that very few labor leaders are reasonable and responsive	52	49	47	52
Opinion of big business corporations Percentage whose opinion of big business corporations is unfavorable	34	36	32	32
Would you favor higher taxes to increase police protection? **Percentage who favor**	35	32	35	36
Would you welcome lowering property taxes in the spirit of California's Proposition 13? **Percentage who favor**	70	70	69	65
Would you advocate cutting all taxes by one-third? **Percentage who favor**	46	49	49	49
Would you approve trying to control inflation by freezing all salaries and wages? **Percentage who favor**	39	42	45	39
Would you approve trying to control inflation by limiting income increases to 5%? **Percentage who favor**	41	39	37	37
Do you think the growth of big business is becoming a threat to the American way of life? **Percentage in agreement**	27	34	36	51
Do you feel that the cost of living has gone up more rapidly than your income? **Percentage in agreement**	90	79	70	52

SOURCE: Roper Reports, 1978.

such as environmental questions, energy, and economic growth—lack any real connection with the old liberal-conservative axis. What is the liberal response on a "trade-off" question of environmental protection versus economic growth? Upper and lower economic groups split only on interests that hit close to home. For example, more low-income Americans favor the elimination of pollution-control devices on cars to save gasoline than do people with high incomes; but at the same time they are less willing to approve special taxes on "gas-guzzling" cars. The common thread here, of course, is that the less affluent are less prepared to pay the price of environmental cleanup.

Even as Americans endorse measures to restrict the growth of government spending, however, they remain extraordinarily supportive of a high level of government services in virtually all sectors. Again, there are no significant class differences in this commitment. Thus almost identical proportions of business managers and unskilled workers, of high-income people and those in the lowest income brackets, want to maintain or even increase current spending for the environment, health, urban needs, education, improving the position of blacks, and the like.

While Americans rich and poor overwhelmingly approve the "service state," they no less decisively view inflation as National Enemy No. 1. Without any notable differences by economic position, they want to curtail taxing, spending, and the recourse to federal budgetary deficits, which they hold responsible for inflation. In the fall of 1978, an extraordinary 76 percent of all Americans—three-quarters of business and professional people and three-quarters of manual workers—described inflation as the nation's "most important problem."

Since political leaders naturally respond to the same environment as the general public, more and more of them are struggling with the dilemma of continuing to support a large government role—while hammering down its inflationary cost. This was brought out clearly in a series of interviews with political leaders in California, where the future typically seems to come a little sooner than elsewhere. Such a veteran of Democratic politics as State Treasurer Jesse Unruh sums up: "Most of us have finally come to subscribe to the conservative thesis that government spending is itself a prime cause of inflation, and so we are scurrying around now trying to do what conservatives have been saying for thirty years should be done." But he makes clear that neither he nor (in his opinion) the voters want a retreat from the interventionist thrusts of modern government.

On the Republican front in California politics, former Governor Ronald Reagan can plausibly boast of his own early appreciation of the need to combine commitments to both government services and government restraint. In a recent interview, he cited again his own gubernatorial record of (1) raising welfare grants to the "truly needy" by 43 percent, while (2) saving some $2 billion through effective management, which removed from the welfare rolls those not entitled to such benefits.

A good deal of this new ideological mix had its social origins in the burgeoning national prosperity of the first quarter century after World War II. In that span, the median family income of Americans approximately doubled in real purchasing power. The class tensions of the New Deal years became largely smothered in this widespread and increasing affluence. If the big increases in taxation of those years had fallen disproportionately on upper-income groups, the earlier conflicts over public-sector activity might have persisted. But instead, between 1953 and 1977, the proportion of income paid in taxes *doubled* for the average family—while increasing by only *50 percent* among families earning four times the national average. The costs of government were thus brought home forcefully to a broad range of the populace.

Whether or not the perception squares with reality, the lower socioeconomic groups now feel they have been specially victimized by inflation. Thus 90 percent of those earning $7,000 a year or less—but only 52 percent of those with family incomes over $25,000—claimed in late 1978 that the rising cost of living was outrunning their income growth.

This sense of inflation as a "democratic" enemy, striking

PROPORTIONS OF FAMILY INCOME
PAID IN TAXES, 1953–1977

	1953	1966	1977
Families earning around the average income	11.8%	17.8%	22.5%
Families earning twice the average income	16.5	19.3	24.8
Families earning four times the average income	20.2	23.4	31.4

Source: Advisory Commission on Inter-governmental Relations.

the great masses of the society, has had a profound impact on the citizenry's attitudes toward government. And since the lower income and occupation groups see themselves as especially burdened by inflation, they support "anti-government" actions at least as heartily as the once instinctively anti-government upper-middle class. In the wake of all this, the old thrusts of public debate have become changed—and confused.

To be sure, there still are liberals and conservatives of the pure New Deal species. But they have lost their mass followings. Yet to come is an even ruder awakening, however, for conservative activists who have long pursued the Holy Grail of an "emerging conservative majority" and who now imagine that this era of "taxpayers' revolt" promises their triumph. Lewis Uhler, the former Reagan aide who heads the National Tax-Limitation Committee, speaks optimistically of the currently popular amendments to limit taxing and spending as a "vehicle for reeducation" of a public too long in the thrall of liberal doctrines. "People approach this thing as a dollars-and-cents issue, but after you discuss it a bit they come to recognize that the broader question involves the distribution of power. Are we going to have collective, state-centralized, political decisions? Or are we going to have market decisions?"

But there is no indication whatsoever that the general public will respond to this brand of traditional conservative preachment. In matters of economic policy, Americans now seem beyond the classic liberal-conservative argument. To want a high level of government services—without a serious inflationary impact—is neither liberal nor conservative. The citizens may not get what they want—and some would argue that their goals are inherently unattainable—but in the vernacular of our day, this is "where they are coming from."

What has become clear is the direct and fundamental relationship between the rise of a new set of issues and American social and economic development. In its advanced industrial era, the nation has experienced a tremendous growth of the white-collar and professional-technical work force, the relative decline of agriculture and manufacturing, the rise of the knowledge and information sectors of the economy—and the unprecedented expansion of higher education.

Thus propelled, the pace of cultural change has quickened more than at any time since the late nineteenth century, when the country shifted from a rural and agricultural to an urban and industrial base. The main reason for the present-day prominence of cultural issues is the sheer size of the population that is now trained in the use of symbols and occupied with producing them. With its educated and relatively leisured citizenry, its elaborate communications systems, and its massive institutions involved in cultural innovation and interpretation, this society almost inevitably spawns conflict around the relative receptivity—or hostility—of different groups to changes in social and cultural values.

Should women assume new roles? Should individual preference and choice take precedence over the older moral strictures against premarital sex, divorce, abortion, and the like? Should such bourgeois values as hard work and frugality give way to greater emphasis on personal fulfillment and self-expression? And should modern culture itself—built around the belief that the individual, and not any institution, is the ultimate source of moral judgment—be pursued vigorously to its logical conclusions?

A common theme runs through all of these issues, and the public divides on them in a remarkably consistent fashion. American higher education teaches that modernity is to be welcomed, not resisted. So it is hardly surprising that college-educated people are those most receptive to virtually every facet of social and cultural change, while the grade-school-trained populace—least exposed to the scientific and rationalist outlook—is the most resistant.

The graph on page 39 on various social issues shows that receptivity to new values and practices climbs steadily with each upward step on the educational ladder. This holds to such an extent that people with post-bachelor's training give greater endorsement to virtually every feature of contemporary social change than do those with just a bachelor's degree—while the latter in turn welcome change more enthusiastically than persons with only one to three years' formal college training, and so on down the educational line. No other factor—occupation, income, race, religion, ethnic background, or geographic region—matches this extraordinary impact of education.

All this suggests an emergence of "social class" in a new form. This is not a term to be used casually. Broad common grounds of interests and values, accruing from position in the social structure, must be present before the designation of a "class" is made. But classes do not need to be defined by size of income or type of job. In a national setting of extensive cultural change, social classes can emerge just as naturally around levels of education as they once did around levels of income.

The new class differences manifest themselves in varied ways—some of which can seem confounding. For example: since business values are part of the traditional American culture, college-educated managers and professionals are now more critical and challenging of business than are high-school-trained manual workers. This really is "Karl Marx upside down."

Quite pragmatic group interests also sometimes intrude. For example: college-educated Americans support civil rights more than their grade-school counterparts, not simply because their educational experience has so inclined them, but also because they are more remote from the "front lines" of

THE NEW SOCIAL AND CULTURAL DIVISIONS

Today's serious class differences strikingly revolve not around economic questions but around social and cultural issues. With a new kind of consistence, these differences hinge on educational experience—with the college-trained proving more "liberal" than citizens with less education.

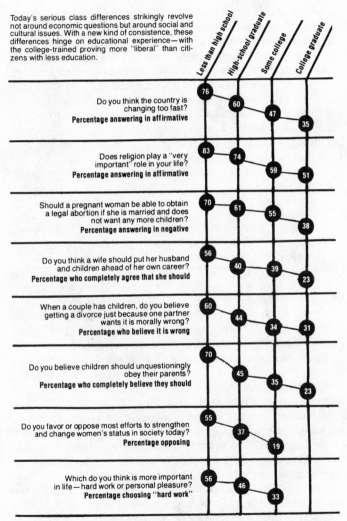

Do you think the country is changing too fast?
Percentage answering in affirmative
76 · 60 · 47 · 35

Does religion play a "very important" role in your life?
Percentage answering in affirmative
83 · 74 · 59 · 51

Should a pregnant woman be able to obtain a legal abortion if she is married and does not want any more children?
Percentage answering in negative
70 · 61 · 55 · 38

Do you think a wife should put her husband and children ahead of her own career?
Percentage who completely agree that she should
56 · 40 · 39 · 23

When a couple has children, do you believe getting a divorce just because one partner wants it is morally wrong?
Percentage who believe it is wrong
60 · 44 · 34 · 31

Do you believe children should unquestioningly obey their parents?
Percentage who completely believe they should
70 · 45 · 35 · 23

Do you favor or oppose most efforts to strengthen and change women's status in society today?
Percentage opposing
55 · 37 · 19

Which do you think is more important in life—hard work or personal pleasure?
Percentage choosing "hard work"
56 · 46 · 33

Column headings: Less than high school · High-school graduate · Some college · College graduate

SOURCES: *Time*/Yankelovich, Skelly, and White, 1977-78; General Social Survey, National Opinion Research Center, 1978; Roper Reports, 1978; and the Los Angeles *Times*, 1978.

racial change. It is simply less costly for them to adopt an accommodating posture vis-à-vis black demands.

There is a natural inclination, to which this author has at times yielded, to stay with familiar labels and try to apply them promiscuously to new situations. But this is a vain exercise. Support for women's rights, abortion, fewer restrictions on divorce, the right to use marijuana if one chooses, individual choice in sexual conduct—these really are not "liberal" in the New Deal usage. There is simply no necessary philosophical linkage between the liberal political economy of the New Deal and the advocacy of liberal cultural change.

In such a political season as this, therefore, there is nothing surprising about a young Democratic governor, heir to a tradition of New Deal liberalism, espousing constitutional restrictions on public spending and taxation—while at the same time taking a generally liberal position on social and cultural questions. A lot of Americans occupy precisely this ideological position. The future of Jerry Brown, California governor and presidential aspirant, is by no means clear. What is clear is that the Brown approach is not captious or idiosyncratic.

As the federal deficit has soared, and as government generally has come to be seen as the initiator of major inflation, the popular outcry has become ever louder. But this new clamor is wholly different from the old conservative aversion to governmental activity per se. Government will not be cut back, and something of an equilibrium is likely to be reached between taxing and spending on the one hand and the overall rate of economic growth.

While social and cultural change always generates strong resistance, the public support for such change has steadily increased of late. The prudent politician will recognize this. One will not win many foreseeable elections by assuming that the American people are swinging "to the right." They are not. In the whole area of cultural change, the public on the whole has been moving toward a more liberal stance.

As for working-class Americans, they will be significantly less receptive to new liberal economic appeals than in the past—and they will be decidedly more resistant to cultural change than their more prosperous, better-educated fellow citizens. While they will not repudiate New Deal liberalism, they will be the least venturesome part of the populace. Instead, the higher-status Americans can be expected to be the proponents of any new government initiatives. Often these proponents will be joined by ethnic groups, especially blacks and Hispanics, with a strong sense of group deprivation. And in this context, the outlines of a "top-bottom" alliance against the social "middle" will continue to operate, albeit as loosely and incompletely as in the past.

Finally, the most peculiar and striking mark of these developments is the way in which they are intruding upon the lives of the nation's two major political parties. They are not affecting the relative strength of the Democrats and the Republicans—but they are diminishing the effective power of *both*. As Jesse Unruh says: "The Democratic party is a very malleable instrument, and we are much better at plagiarism, and much more flexible, than the Republicans." For whatever reason, the Democrats in fact have picked up on the main currents of ideological change and are beginning to articulate them. So the massive alteration in the essential nature of political conflict is occurring without much threat to Democratic ascendancy.

But Democrats and Republicans alike face grave difficulties as they try to make some coherent aggregate out of the new cultural issues in order to build majority coalitions. Because these issues turn on pivotal social values, they stubbornly resist traditional formulas or stratagems for political compromise. Instead, they lend themselves far more to the absolutist or moralistic appeals that distinguish "single issue" politics.

It is not surprising, then, that this style of politics so clearly appears in the ascendant. It is indeed a new game in town. And a major reason for its popularity is the fact that it is much harder to apply old-style coalition politics to the cultural issues that now divide us than to the New Deal economic issues that once—more cleanly and more neatly—split the American electorate.

CRISIS OF THE PARTY SYSTEM[3]

I

Something has gone badly wrong with the American party system. All gauges register trouble. The steady decline in voter turnout, the steady increase in ticket-splitting, the multiplication of voters styling themselves independents, the growing tendency of candidates to conceal rather than emphasize party affiliation, the substitution of television for party organization, the rise of personalist political movements—these are surely characteristics of a party system in an advanced state of decay.

Many observers, moreover, see the decay of the parties as a basic cause of the larger crisis of ungovernability. Historically, it is said, the party has brought disparate voters together into coherent combinations, contained explosive issues through brokerage and compromise and provided the means of concerted action in a government based on the separation of powers. With the party system no longer channeling the energies of our politics, these energies shoot off in all directions, and nothing gets done at the center.

Many factors are adduced to explain this crisis. I would like to offer an historian's thoughts as to what the crisis is *not* about and then as to what, in my judgment, it *is* about.

We hear, for example, that supposedly novel and untoward developments—the fragmentation of Congress, the power of lobbies, the spread of single-issue movements—help account for the decline of the parties. One wonders whether these phenomena are really all that novel, and whether their existence explains very much.

[3] Excerpted from a two-part newspaper article by Arthur Schlesinger Jr., Albert Schweitzer Professor of the Humanities, City University of New York; winner of Pulitzer Prizes in history and biography; and a member of the *Wall Street Journal*'s Board of Contributors. *Wall Street Journal.* p 30. My. 10, '79; p 20. My. 14, '79. Reprinted by permission of *The Wall Street Journal.* Copyright © 1979 Dow Jones & Company, Inc. All rights reserved.

Lapse From a Golden Age?

Take Congress. Columnists write weighty pieces implying that the current incorrigibility on Capitol Hill represents a terrible lapse from some golden age when legislators unquestioningly obeyed party whips. But there never was such a golden age. Even Franklin Roosevelt, in the era of the so-called rubberstamp Congresses, had to fight for every New Deal measure after the Hundred Days and, with all his craft and popularity, was not uncommonly defeated on cherished initiatives, such as discretionary neutrality and the Supreme Court.

Nor was party indiscipline new in the days of FDR. It is inherent in the American political order. Partly because of the constitutional separation of powers, partly because of the size and diversity of the country, American political parties, as Tocqueville observed 140 years ago, "are impatient of control and are never manageable except in moments of great public danger."

This innate unmanageability, Tocqueville pointed out, resulted from the dependence of the legislator on his constituents.

A representative [he wrote] is never sure of his supporters, and, if they forsake him, he is left without a resource. . . . Thus it is natural that in democratic countries the members of political assemblies should think more of their constituents than of their party. . . . But what ought to be said to gratify constituents is not always what ought to be said in order to serve the party to which representatives profess to belong.

Party indiscipline, far from being a novelty of our own fallen times, is one of the conditions that American democracy has endured from the start.

The same reflection applies to the theory of lobbies as some new and ghastly menace to the republic. We have had lobbies ever since we have had Congress. And lobbies were never more powerful than in those years after the Civil War when we came as near as we ever have to the beatitude of party discipline. Those who think that private-interest lobbies are a horrid invention of the late 20th Century ought to read "The Gilded Age" by Mark Twain and Charles Dudley Warner (1873) or meditate the gaudy career of Sam Ward (1814–1884), the King of the Lobby. On the other hand, the public-interest lobby has never been more effective than it is today; and to some degree this development offsets the private interest groups. Ralph Nader is the modern response to Colonel Sellers and Sam Ward.

Nor are single-issue movements the appalling innovation that columnists, contemplating the anti-abortionists, the anti-gun-controllers, the ecologists, the homosexuals, and so on, evidently suppose them to be. What Madison called the "mischiefs of faction" has been an abiding concern in American history. Single-issue movements have flickered across the political landscape from 1787 to 1979, whether devoted to the extirpation of Freemasonry, the abolition of slavery, the restriction of immigration, the issuance of greenbacks or the enactment of prohibition. American democracy has survived these movements too.

When the Know-Nothing party was at its height, Horace Greeley predicted accurately that it would "run its career rapidly, and vanish as suddenly as it appeared. It *may* last through the next presidential canvass; but hardly longer than that. . . . It would seem as devoid of the elements of persistence as an anti-cholera or an anti-potato-rot party would be." The Know-Nothings, it should be noted, had a far greater success in elections than any of the one-eyed movements of our own day have had. . . .

II

In an earlier piece I suggested that the chronic afflictions of the party system—congressional fragmentation, lobbies, single-issue movements—can be overcome, as they have been in the past, by competent presidential leadership. The reason for the deep and perhaps incurable crisis of the system lies elsewhere. It lies above all in the organic changes wrought in the political environment by the electronic revolution.

The party system had already begun to lose historic functions well before the advent of electronic technology. The decline of immigration deprived the political organization of its classic clientele. The rise of civil service limited its patronage. The New Deal took over its welfare role. But today two modern electronic devices—television and the computer—are having a devastating and possibly fatal impact on the traditional structure of American politics.

The traditional structure had three tiers: the politician, the voter and, in between, a cluster of intermediate agencies—most significantly the party organization; but also the trade association, the labor union, the farm organization, the ethnic brotherhood—negotiating between the politician and the voter, interceding for each on behalf of the other and providing the links that held the party system together.

The electronic revolution has abolished the mediatorial function. Television presents the politician directly to the voter, who makes his judgment more on what Walter Cronkite and John Chancellor show him than on what the party leaders tell him. Moreover, television, as Austin Ranney suggests, has become the main source not just of information but of "reality" for the voter.

At the same time, computerized public opinion polling presents the voter directly to the politician, who judges opinion more by what the polls show him than by what the party leaders tell him. The political organization is left to wither on the vine.

The organization has thus lost its domination of the lines of information and communication between government and public opinion. It has lost most of its power to select top candidates too. This loss is often blamed on the spread of presidential primaries. But presidential primaries have been around for a long time. It took television to transform them into the controlling force they are today. Television has given the ordinary citizen a new sense of entitlement in the political process. Presidential nominations are no longer settled by

party leaders in smoke-filled rooms but by primaries and caucuses at the grassroots. Political conventions have become
ceremonies of ratification. A person born the last year that a
convention required more than one ballot to nominate a presidential candidate would be 27 years old today.

"Photo Opportunities"

Television stimulates political activism. Every rebel
group knows about "photo opportunities" and schemes to get
itself on camera. What Sam Lubell has called the "struggle
for political visibility" is the means by which a newly demanding electorate presses its claims. All this has further
weakened party identification and intensified the distrust of
politicians and organizations—a distrust that, substantiated
by spectacular policy disgraces at home and abroad, has
turned into rabid hostility.

Political loyalties, once as sacred as religious affiliations,
are steadily facing away. Campaign billboards in our hetero-
dox age play down the party of the candidate—a profound
change from the time when Thomas B. Reed [Republican
Speaker of the House, 1890s] could say, "A good party is better than the best man that ever lived."

The party organization is in addition losing its control
over campaigns. Television and polling have bred a new profession of electronic manipulators. Assembled in election-
management firms, the media specialists, working indif-
ferently for one party or the other, reduce campaigns to
displays not of content but of technique.

Can the traditional party system be saved? I must confess
skepticism about many of the proposed remedies. The sug-
gestion is made, for example, that party professionals be allocated a fixed proportion of seats in nominating conventions,
that campaign funds should go to party organizations rather
than to individual candidates and that other guarantees
should be sought for party organizations against the depreda-
tions of electronic mercenaries, on the one hand, and citizen
activists, on the other.

Some of these proposals seem to me doubtful on the merits. It is hard to justify the proposition that the interests of American democracy would have been better served through history had political funds been entrusted to party bosses rather than to issue-oriented candidates. Let us not in our adversity succumb to a romantic myth of party organization. New ideas have won access to politics precisely through crusaders like T.R., Wilson, F.D.R., who had to take the party away from the organization in order to move the nation ahead. The crusaders were responsive to needs and issues; the bosses to boodle and survival.

Nor are larger proposals to centralize and discipline the parties more persuasive. This effort is against the grain of American parties, for reasons observed long since by Tocqueville, as well as against the spirit of the electronic age.

Nor is discipline necessarily all that transcendent a virtue. The reputation of Congress was never lower than in the second half of the 19th Century when parties were most disciplined. Those were the times that led Mark Twain to write: "Reader, suppose you were an idiot. And suppose you were a member of Congress. But I repeat myself."

Strict party discipline is likely to mean a preponderance of idiots following the leadership like sheep. My guess is that we have had in recent Congresses fewer idiots and more informed, educated and independent-minded legislators than we have had since the early Republic. But the price we pay for independent-minded legislators is their determination to make up their own minds. We can't have it both ways—a high-quality Congress and sheeplike discipline. The improvement in quality also explains, I would think, the increased defection rate, for there are fewer time-servers today and more people who, coming to Congress to accomplish things, then retire in frustration when they discover that they are not getting very far.

Some political scientists blame the decline of the parties on the reform movements of the last decade. But party reform was a response, not a cause. Many of the "reforms"—the modernization of procedures, for example, and the larger representation of women and blacks—strengthened the parties. Other "reforms" carelessly or deliberately ignored the interests of parties as institutions. But the idea that procedural reforms caused the crisis, or that repealing these reforms will cure it, is akin to the delusion of Rostand's Chanticleer that his cock-a-doodle made the sun rise.

Obviously we should do what we can to avoid weakening the party system further. Such proposals as the direct election of Presidents, a national primary, a national initiative and referendum, might well administer the *coup de grace* and must be resisted. The provision of free television time to the national party committees would be modestly useful in propping the parties up. But most structural remedies are beside the point. The attempt to shore up structure against loss of function is artificial and futile.

Restoration of Serious Function

The party system is simply no longer effective as an agency of mass mobilization, or as an agency of candidate selection, or as an agency of information and communication, or as an agency of brokerage, or as an agency of welfare and acculturation, or as an expression of the political culture. It can be saved only by the restoration of serious function. At present, the party organization does little more than certify platforms and provide labels for the organization of elections and legislature.

Two things alone can give these decrepit parties a lease on life: the incubation of ideas that give promise of meeting the hard questions of our age, especially inflation and energy; and the election of competent Presidents who will thereafter act to revitalize their parties in the presidential interest. The best hope for the party is as an instrument of Presidents who need to overcome the separation of powers and to mobilize mass support in order to put new programs into effect.

Otherwise we may be beginning a slow, confused descent into an era of what Walter Dean Burnham has called "politics without parties." Political adventurers will roam the countryside like Chinese warlords or Iranian ayatollahs, recruiting personal armies, conducting hostilities against some rival warlords and forming alliances with others, and, as they win elections, striving to govern through ad hoc coalitions in legislatures.

The prospect is not inviting. The crumbling away of the historic parties would leave political power in America concentrated in the adventurers, in the interest groups that finance them and in the executive bureaucracy. The rest of us might not have even the limited entry into and leverage on the process that the party system, for all its defects, has made possible. Without parties, our politics would grow angrier, wilder and more irresponsible.

Still we cannot restore the past by act of will. "The sum of political life," wrote Henry Adams, "was, or should have been the attainment of a working political system. Society needed to reach it. If moral standards broke down, and machinery stopped working, new morals and machinery of some sort had to be invented." This seems to be our problem—not to engage in artificial resuscitation of a system that has served its time but to invent the morals, machinery and ideas required for the last quarter of the 20th Century.

THE DECLINE OF THE PARTY IN AMERICAN ELECTIONS[4]

[The] decline of [American political parties] can be easily noticed if we briefly review the position parties held in the electoral process through most of American history, even as recently as the end of World War II. Parties then typically

[4] Excerpted from article by Gerald M. Pomper. *Political Science Quarterly.* 92:23–41. Spring 1977. The article, adapted from the author's essay "The Decline of Partisan Politics," is reprinted from *The Impact of the Electoral Process*, Sage Electoral Studies Yearbook, Vol. 3, Louis Maisel and Joseph Cooper, editors, copyright 1977, p 13–38, by permission of the publisher, Sage Publications, Inc. (Beverly Hills/London). Gerald M. Pomper is professor and chairman of the department of political science at Rutgers University; senior research associate of the Center for Policy Research; and author of *Voters' Choice, Elections in America*, and *The Election of 1976*.

possessed either legal or practical monopolies of three vital factors: legitimacy, resources, and recruitment.

The legitimacy of parties was evident in the loyalties expressed by the voters. Americans were fiercely loyal to the two major parties, whatever their labels in any particular historical era. Most voters retained the same party attachments throughout life. Although periodically disrupted at times of critical realignment, even these realignments could be explained more by generational change than individual conversion.

The depth of affection could be located in political humor, which abounds in stories such as that of the Irish family in Boston in which all the children developed well, except for the black sheep who became a Republican. It can be found in the accounts of the "militaristic" period of the nineteenth century, in which partisans were as devoted to the Republican and Democratic standards as their fathers in the Civil War had been loyal to the Union and Confederacy. It can be found in the aggregate election statistics, in which communities returned virtually the same vote for each faction year after year, and ticket splitting or "drop off" in the vote at one end of the very long ballot was almost undetectable. It can be found in modern survey data, in which up to 90 percent of the national samples of the 1950s identified consistently and openly with the major parties.

Parties classically possessed not only legitimacy, but resources. One resource was access to the ballot itself, as the formal rules (written by party-dominated state legislatures) essentially eliminated nonparty candidates, even after adoption of the Australian ballot. Campaigning resources were also controlled by the parties, most evidently when precinct canvassing and turnout were the principal means of winning votes. The financing needed for elections was another party resource, with money raised and spent by party committees or individuals closely associated with these organizations, and independent organizations existing largely as means to evade unrealistic and unenforceable spending ceilings. Patronage provided a means of supplying and multiplying these resources. Spoilsmen reinforced the party monopoly of governmental positions, campaigned for the organization, and contributed to its coffers.

The channels of political recruitment were also dominated by the parties. For most governmental offices in the United States, distinct ladders of political advancement could be located, with the rungs of the ladder held together by the party organizations. Distinct regional patterns could be found as well, such as the apprenticeship system practiced by the Chicago Democratic organization. In the Senate, in the ten-year period after . . . World War II, only 9 percent came to the body without previous political office. Party domination of recruitment was evident in the highest office, the presidency, as well. Except for victorious generals, every national candidate advanced through a number of party positions before receiving his nomination. Precise rules of "availability" existed and served to explain "why great men are not elected president." (James Bryce, *The American Commonwealth,* 3d ed., 1914)

Party domination of the presidential electoral process was based on these monopolies of legitimacy, resources, and recruitment. It can be illustrated by the nominations of 1932, the last year before the modern period of presidential races. In the incumbent Republican party, President Herbert Hoover was easily renominated despite his ineffectiveness in coping with the Great Depression. In control of executive patronage, he was able to keep the state parties in line and to ignore the signs of popular discontent evident in the few, and ineffective, state primaries. . . .

The Modern Electoral Process

The contrast of this historical sketch with the modern election of the president is so great that we are really dealing not simply with a changed system, but an essentially different process. The differences are evident in five aspects: recruitment, strategies of nomination, campaign finance, national conventions, and electoral behavior. In each, considerable change has already occurred, and the effect of these changes is likely to be further deterioration of the parties in the future. . . .

Presidential recruitment has changed in both its character and its sources. Campaigns for the White House now begin essentially through a process of self-selection and depend for their success on the development of organizations personally bound to the candidate. . . .

The presidential nominating campaign has been nationalized. No longer is it true that there are no national parties, only fifty state parties, as the old textbook cliché read. At least for the presidency it would be more accurate to say that there are no state parties, and perhaps no national parties as well. The state parties have largely and deliberately written themselves out of the presidential nomination. Beset by new and complex rules for the selection of delegates, many state organizations have simply left the choice and mandate of convention delegates to state primaries.

The parties' place has been taken by candidate organizations. As campaigners, these candidate organizations are far different from the locally centered groups of the traditional state parties. By the 1976 campaign, canvassing itself was being handled by out-of-staters. Hundreds of Georgians went to New Hampshire to campaign for Jimmy Carter, while large numbers of Michiganders rang Florida doorbells for President Gerald Ford. That this "carpetbagging" drew little attention and no criticism is quietly impressive evidence of the nationalization of the nominating process, and of its separation from local influences.

Other large national forces are affecting the nominations. A principal means of campaigning is through the mass media. The standing of candidates is now certified not by their support among party leaders or their particular office but by a small group of reporters and commentators for newspapers, magazines, and television. "They are acknowledged experts, well connected in political circles throughout the land. Their reports appear in the nation's most prestigious newspapers and respected news broadcasts. . . . Collectively they are what columnist Russell Baker has called 'the Great Mention-iser,' the source of self-fulfilling stories that a person has been 'mentioned' as a possible presidential nominee." (W. Keech and D. Matthews, *The Party's Choice*, 1976)

The national strategies of candidates are directed toward winning the notice of "the Great Mentioniser" and of the press generally, and then gaining more widespread public attention. Various tactics will be used to win this attention, since public opinion, and its measurement in the national polls, is usually decisive. Vital issues may be emphasized, as McGovern stressed Vietnam in 1972; or primary victories may be employed to demonstrate an attractive personality, as Carter did in 1976. Whatever the tactics employed, however, their common feature is that they depend little for their success on the support of party organizations.

Standing in the public opinion polls has become decisive in winning presidential nominations. With conspicuous exceptions, such as McGovern and Carter, the leader in the national polls before the primaries almost always goes on to win designation. Furthermore, it is virtually certain that the preconvention poll leader, even an insurgent such as McGovern or Carter, will be victorious in his party. To be sure, poll standings are affected by primaries and by direct support of the state parties, "but the strongest relations are the long-run effects in the opposite direction—the effects of national opinion on winning both the state primary elections and the presidential nomination." (J. R. Beninger, *Public Opinion Quarterly*, Spring 1976)

Candidates appeal to geographically diffuse constituencies, not to areal coalitions. The constituencies may be McGovern's opponents of the Vietnam war, or Ronald Reagan's ideological conservatives, or Carter's seekers for governmental purity, or Henry Jackson's laborites. Their common feature is their lack of local coloring. The diminishing impact of geography can also be seen in the convention decisions themselves. Until recently, there was a stable voting structure in both parties, in which the states could be consistently ordered along a single dimension. In the Republican party, factions could be arrayed geographically and ideologically, from conservative to liberal.... Conservative candidates such as Robert Taft or Barry Goldwater received their support from the same end of this spectrum (largely southern and midwestern) and liberals from the other end (largely eastern). In the Democratic party, with the direction reversed, liberals received most support from the Midwest and Far West, conservatives from the South. This structure has not been evident since 1964....

Political Money

The decline of established partisan politics is further promoted by developments in campaign finance, most particularly the post-Watergate reform acts of 1974 and 1976. The full effects of the laws will not be known for some time, and they will certainly be different from both the intentions of Congress and the expectations of academic observers. The general effect, however, is already apparent. It is to shift money, the most vital resource of politics, from the parties to the control of individual candidates and to nonparty individuals and groups.

The new law, supplemented by the Supreme Court's interpretive decision of 1976, takes money away from the parties, while it provides finances for individuals and outside agencies. The parties are deprived of money by the limitations on individual contributors who may not give more than $1000 to any single recipient. The total amount of spending by a candidate or party is also limited. While the national party may spend $3 million, its presidential candidate is limited to $20 million, plus adjustments and fund-raising expenses. While these restrictions are easily justified as means of preventing corruption, their effect is to limit politicians rather than to restrict electoral spending generally.

In fact, the law and the Supreme Court do not limit the influence of money in elections—but rather only the influence of party money. Four aspects of the legislation are particularly important. Existing provisions provide for federal subsidies for campaigning, but these subsidies are paid to candidates, not to parties. With the candidates provided seven times the capital that is permitted parties, this provision promotes the increasing separation of national candidates from the parties. Furthermore, subsidies are paid only to presidential candidates, leaving the rest of the party from Congress to local office fiscally unrelated to the head of the ticket. As interpreted by the Supreme Court, moreover, even the limitations on spending may be ignored by a candidate who declines federal subsidies and raises his own funds. Therefore, candidates of personal wealth or with close connections to such wealth—e.g., a Rockefeller or Kennedy—can still spend unlimited sums. Finally, there is no limitation on contributions or expenditures "independent" of the candidates and parties. Therefore individuals or groups are free to raise and spend whatever they wish, so long as they do not become allied to the political parties. It now becomes ever more to the advantage of political interests to ignore established politicians.

This legislation may become the classic illustration of the dominance of latent over manifest functions. We may doubt that Congress intended to subvert the political parties, but this is the cumulative impact of the finance law. It provides a sufficient explanation of the astounding Republican contest of 1976. The conventional wisdom of politics—and political science—cannot explain the near-success of Ronald Reagan. An incumbent president, however chosen, should easily win renomination. In the beginning of the election year, President Ford had achieved a measure of personal popularity; the Vietnam war had ended; there were signs of economic expansion; and the president had the support of almost all important party officials. Compared to Herbert Hoover's position in 1932, there was no reason to doubt his convention success. Nevertheless, Reagan persevered, and the availability of money must be considered a major reason for his persistence. Regardless of party pressure or early primary defeats, Reagan could continue to count on personal contributions, which were doubled in value by federal subsidies. He further

benefited from independent expenditures by his sympathiz-
ers. The national government thus subsidized insurgency
against its own chief executive.

In the Democratic party, with no incumbent leader, the
law promoted factionalism, providing support for all comers,
regardless of their standing in the party or chances of success.
George Wallace, who split the party in 1968, gained propor-
tionately the most federal subsidies, while even Ellen McCor-
mack, running in opposition to the platform, became eligible
for federal grants. The Supreme Court's suspension of the law
during the vital primary period also affected the race, leaving
Morris Udall in debt while allowing Carter, a relatively
wealthy candidate, to raise funds privately.

The finance laws reinforce the other developments we
have noted. They provide support for the personal, candi-
date-oriented organizations which now dominate presidential
politics. They demand a national constituency, since funds
must be raised in at least twenty states to be eligible for federal matching. By ignoring and slighting parties, they promote the general tendencies to emphasize other means of
campaigning. They stimulate appeals to ideological and interest groups. Together, surely, these changes do not promote
anything resembling a "responsible two-party system."
Rather, they foster the turn toward "antiparty government."

The Decline of Conventions

New finance laws have accelerated another trend, the
elimination of the party nominating convention as a significant decision-making body. No convention since 1952 has
taken more than a single ballot to nominate its presidential
candidate. Throughout this period, moreover, with the exception of the 1976 Republican confrontation, the winner of
the nomination has been determined before the convention
actually convened. Only large blunders could have prevented
the nominations of such front-runners as Kennedy in 1960 or
Nixon in 1968, even though there was a spurious excitement
to these meetings.

Once described as "a chess game disguised as a circus," the convention now resembles more a newspaper chess column in which amateurs replay the moves of past masters. Among the reasons for this decline of the convention is the loss of political expertise. The participants at these conclaves never acquired the skill to conduct grand negotiations, or have lost this ability through disuse. Like all talents, that of striking political deals requires practice, but contemporary convention delegates and their leaders have no experience upon which to draw. Even the few survivors of a bygone age, such as the late Mayor Richard J. Daley, find their skills atrophied through disuse. Surely the Democratic conventions of 1968 and 1972 were ideal occasions for the emergence of a compromise or dark-horse candidate, such as Edward Kennedy. Yet, in both years, the party's leaders fumbled away the opportunity to choose this likely winner. . . .

The critical agencies in presidential nominations have changed. One of the most vital is the mass media, which appraise candidates, their abilities, and their chances of success. Candidates use the media to appeal directly to vital constituencies, rather than bargaining with party representatives. The media's particular interest in news results in the exaggeration of the importance of discrete events, and their interpretation of these events defines reality. Thus, the New Hampshire primary has been transformed from a minor test of popularity in a minor state to the event which gives a candidate "momentum." Television has further contributed to the decline of the convention by making classic negotiations virtually impossible, for "open covenants openly arrived at" are as difficult to achieve domestically as internationally. Parties do not want to present a messy picture of bargaining to their costless television audience. Instead they seek to present an image of unity and concord, and the result is dullness and impotence.

Party power over nominations has also been displaced by the spread of state primaries which mandate delegate votes. As recently as the 1960s, primaries elected fewer than one-third of the delegates and were useful largely as confirmations of the candidates' popular standing and electoral appeal. By 1976, nearly three-fourths of the delegates were chosen in these contests, and they had become decisive. A candidate carrying most, not necessarily all, of the primaries, would win the nomination as did McGovern and Carter. The convention could retain some power of decision only if the voters were clearly divided, as in the Reagan-Ford confrontation. The odds surely are against recurrence of this latter pattern. By removing the party organizations from the nominations, state presidential primaries sever the head of the political party's body—a dangerous condition.

Voters and Parties

Electoral behavior provides the final evidence of the decline of the parties. The organized parties have less influence because they have less value to candidates. To win a presidential nomination once brought an aspirant not only ballot position, funding, and campaign workers. Most importantly, it assured him of a substantial share of the vote simply on the basis of the Democratic or Republican label he had won. This label is less helpful today, and candidates therefore need pay less to its manufacturers.

The decreased impact of partisanship is abundantly clear. In answers to standard questions on self-identification, one-third to two-fifths of the American electorate now disclaim affective ties to the parties, and the proportion reaches a majority among the youngest voters. There is a general disdain for parties, reflected in the large proportions who see them as contributing little to the maintenance of democratic government. . . .

Loss of Party Functions

. . . Generally, we can say that the electoral success of insurgents demonstrates that the political parties have lost their monopoly over recruitment. This loss is evident beyond the presidential level. The last areas to nominate state candidates through party processes were Connecticut and Indiana, but these bastions have fallen, and nomination through the direct primary is now universal. Even attempts by the party leaders to endorse candidates in the primary are now limited. Where attempted, such efforts are likely to be self-defeating, as in New York, where the party endorsement brings a candidate not votes but the burden of charges of "bossism." Nor are party careers necessary to advancement. The ambitious can switch parties, . . . or be elected as pure independents, . . . or seek high office without previous political experience. . . .

Additionally, the party has lost its monopoly over vital resources. Presidential funds, as we have noted, are now independently provided through the federal government, and the 1976 Democratic platform promises similar support for congressional candidates. George Wallace was able to secure a place on the ballot in all of the fifty states, despite the opposition of both major parties, and the Supreme Court has facilitated access by other independent candidates, such as Eugene McCarthy in 1976. Campaigning is now accomplished not by party canvassers, but through the mass media or, locally, by unions and public employees organizations protected from party patronage demands by civil service laws. Delegates to national conventions are elected on the basis of their candidate preference, not as rewards for their loyalty and service to the organization.

As the parties become less able to control these vital resources of the electoral process, the voters respond less to their weakening appeals. The parties then lose their most vital strength, their very legitimacy. Slogans such as "vote for the man, not the party" come to be descriptions of behavior, not only advertising rhetoric. . . .

The New Party Strength

At the same time as the parties have been weakened by these many tendencies, there has been another, apparently countervailing trend. This is the development of strong national party organizations, evident particularly among the

Democrats. The party has created a coherent set of national institutions and binding rules which sharply contrast with the traditional portrait of the parties as decentralized and incoherent. It is simply no longer true, as [E. E.] Schattschneider wrote in his classic description, that incoherence "constitutes the most important single fact concerning the American parties." (*Party Government*, 1942) Coherence is evident in such indexes as congressional voting, where party unity has recently increased. It is even more evident in party organization. . . .

The party has also created itself as a national body, rather than as a collection of state units. Membership in the national convention is no longer based principally on electoral votes, a reflection of the states as constituent elements, but now equally weights the contribution of these states to a national Democratic vote. Similarly, the national committee once acknowledged state sovereignty by giving equal representation to all states, but now is weighted by the size of states and includes representatives from all branches of federal, state, and local government.

For the first time in American political history, the Democrats in 1974 adopted a national party charter, which gave permanent existence to the party, and provided for mid-term conferences of the party, giving it a visible existence other than during the four days of a presidential nominating convention. New organs of party government were created, including a national finance council, a national education and training council, and a judicial council to settle disputes and interpret party rules. The rudiments of a full governing structure are now in place, including the traditional legislative, executive, and judicial branches.

The national party is able to exercise these powers in the absence of legal constraints. In the 1972 Democratic convention, important credentials disputes turned on the right of the convention to exclude delegates from Illinois and California duly elected under state law. In both instances, these delegates were barred because the credentials committee ruled that they failed to meet some of the new reform rules. A critical decision of the Supreme Court upheld the right of the party to self-government because of "the large public interest in allowing the political processes to function free from judicial supervision." (*O'Brien* v. *Brown*, 1972)

The independence of political parties was further acknowledged in a later case involving the Republicans. A challenge brought against the national party disputed the allocation of convention delegates, arguing for application of the "one-man, one-vote" principle, in the same fashion as the apportionment of state or congressional representatives. The Circuit Court of Appeals, later upheld by the Supreme Court, declined to intervene, declaring the party free to organize "in the way that will make it the most effective organization . . . without interference from the courts." (*Ripon Society* v. *National Republican Party*, 1975)

These decisions are important in themselves for they seem to conflict partially with the earlier position of the Supreme Court which recognized political parties as virtually a formal part of government. It was for this reason that the "white primary" was abolished, even when no state law was involved. In these recent cases, however, the parties are permitted actions which are contrary to state law or which are different from principles of representation applied to formal governmental institutions. The result is to make the parties, at least on the national level, autonomous and potentially strong institutions. At the same time, the parties, as we have argued, are becoming weak influences in the political process. There is a seeming contradiction in the existence of strong institutions of little effectiveness.

The Party as Private Association

The apparent contradiction can be resolved if we recognize that we are witnessing the transformation of American political parties. One element of the transformation is structural, an internal shift of power from state to national parties. While state parties are losing their functions, national parties are developing as coherent organizations. While state parties are not able to control national decisions such as the presidential nomination, national parties are more able to control state decisions such as the selection of convention delegates.

A more basic transformation is occurring as well, altering the place of parties generally in American politics. In the scholarly literature, and even in practice, parties held a special place among the many contestants for power, being recognized as the major intermediate associations between the citizen and the government. While multitudes of interest groups attempted to influence government, the political party was unique as an aggregator of interests, for "no interest group or alliance of such groups has supplanted the party as a device for mobilizing majorities." (D. B. Truman, *The Governmental Process*, 1951)

In contemporary America, it seems more accurate to describe the political party as little more than another private association or interest group. Like other associations, such as the American Medical Association, it attempts to influence elections, but both groups have only marginal effects. Like other associations of a nominally "private" character, it successfully claims independence from governmental regulation. The courts have long been hesitant to interfere with the internal organization of churches or unions. Now the courts have extended similar freedom, based on the same First Amendment principles, to the parties. This reluctance to prescribe party rules suggests that the organization of the Democrats and Republicans is no more politically relevant than the structure of the Episcopal Church or the United Mineworkers.

In elections, the parties are becoming only one of many actors, not the chief contestants. Parties are wooed by ambitious candidates, but so are the mass media. Parties contribute funds to these candidates, but so do private individuals and interest groups. Parties campaign for their nominees, but so do labor unions, and often more widely and more effectively. Parties sponsor candidates, but so do conservationists, business groups, and ideologues of various persuasions.

Even in their most characteristic functions, nominations,

the formal party organizations lack an exclusive position. Delegates to the national conventions are successfully sponsored by these organizations in some places, such as Cook County, Illinois. Success is also achieved by interest groups, such as the 1976 Labor Coalition Clearinghouse, which chose over 400 Democratic delegates, by ideological groups such as New York liberals, and, most decisively, by candidate factions acting outside of or in opposition to the established parties. Once won, a party nomination must be supplemented by endorsements of interest groups, the media, and factional leaders. Eventually, with the increase in electoral instability, a party label on a candidate may come to have no more effect than a union label on clothing.

The nonpreferred position of the parties has now been partially incorporated into federal law. When Congress adopted a revised finance law following the Supreme Court's 1976 decision, a vigorous effort was needed to allow parties to receive contributions in the same manner as other political committees. The final statute does give some particular recognition to the parties, since individuals may contribute up to $20,000 to the parties, while they are limited to $5000 in gifts to other committees. Nevertheless, the law still places the parties in the same juridical position as other private groups, even if it is more well-endowed for purposes of electioneering. However, parties are limited in their spending—giving them a less advantageous position than other committees, which may spend freely.

More generally, the political parties are being incorporated into the overall American system of "interest group liberalism." The liberal model sees politics as a struggle of competing interests. Government is neither to grant privileges nor to handicap any group in this struggle. Government is to be an arbiter, to maintain the competition itself. Its role "is one of ensuring access particularly to the most effectively organized, and of ratifying the agreements and adjustments worked out among the competing leaders and their claims." (T. Lowi, *The End of Liberalism*, 1969)

This model explains many actions of American legislatures and bureaucracies and the character of policy outputs. We now see its application to the electoral process itself. Parties are permitted access, but so are other groups. Government encourages this access through financial subsidies, but no distinction is made among those seeking funds on the basis of their adherence to party principle or discipline. The goal becomes participation for its own sake. Individual participation is encouraged through widespread primaries easily subject to crossovers and insurgencies. Candidate participation is encouraged by easy access to campaign subsidies and "equal time" on the mass media. Group participation is encouraged by permitting independent committees to solicit funds and spread propaganda. New social movements are encouraged through easy placement on the ballot and postelection subsidies. Government does not limit access to the political competition, nor regulate the organization of the competitors, but rather seeks only to stimulate more activity.

The defect of interest group liberalism as a general mode of government is its neglect of policy outcomes. Its application to electoral politics evidences the same defect, for it deprives the parties of a continuing, substantive meaning. Party programs then vary with the character of the particular activists and candidates of a specific time, rather than providing a persisting opportunity for voter judgment. To be sure, the national parties are more organizationally coherent and better able to enforce a measure of internal discipline. What the parties increasingly lack is a palpable reason for coherence and discipline. . . .

Many social trends have promoted the decline of partisan politics in the United States. At root, however, the decline can be traced to a theoretical failure, the placement of the parties within the ideology of interest group liberalism. The place of parties has not been fully considered, even by those most concerned with party reform. These advocates have championed the liberal solution of greater popular involvement in party decisions, while also seeking strengthened national organizations. No contradiction between these aims was seen, as even the notable Schattschneider committee called for both centralized and open parties, arguing, "Clearly such a degree of unity within the parties cannot be brought about without party procedures that give a large body of people an opportunity to share in the development of the party program." (American Political Science Association, "Toward a More Responsible Two-Party System") Today, the contradictions between these two goals are increasingly apparent. Parties can be both hierarchical and participatory only if they are also irrelevant.

The special place of parties must be rethought—and re- claimed. Ultimately, this revival of partisan organizations is properly the concern of advocates of representative government itself. The parties have provided the basic means of aggregating social interests, of simplifying choices for a mass electorate, and of permitting responsibility to be fixed for governmental achievements and failures. They have permitted the voters to make at least a retrospective judgment on public policy and occasionally to provide direction for the future. In the context of the 1976 elections, it is difficult to see these functions being fulfilled. While a Jimmy Carter may enforce unity on the Democrats, this is a personal triumph, implying no permanent responsibility of the party. Among Republicans, the most basic agreement between Ford and Reagan was that neither had any responsibility for the actions of a twice-elected president of their party. Can elections without parties then be anything but short-term choices of particular candidates and their idiosyncratic policies?

The ultimate cost of the decline of parties is the loss of popular control over public policies and the consequent inability of less privileged elements to affect their social fate. "Political parties, with all their well-known human and structural shortcomings, are the only devices thus far invented by the wit of Western man which with some effectiveness can generate countervailing collective power on behalf of the many individually powerless against the relatively few who are individually—or organizationally—powerful." (W. D. Burnham, *Critical Elections and the Mainsprings of American Politics*, 1970) The policy result of party decline will be a fundamental conservatism, with no alternate agency available to generate the political power of a popular majority.

Elections will surely continue, for they have demonstrated their social utility in investing rulers with legitimacy. Social movements will periodically express the discontents of neglected and disadvantaged groups. Grievances will be heard and responded to from time to time by sensitive individual leaders and by legislators concerned over their personal or their constituents' futures. The republican form will persist, even while alienation further develops.

Yet, if the decline of partisan politics continues, if parties become only one among many participants in elections, much will be lost. We may identify the losses as choice, as clarity, as diffuse support, or as the effective aggregation of political interests. But, in a single word, the loss will be that of democracy.

THE DECLINE OF THE PARTIES[5]

The men who do the work of piety and charity in our churches . . . the men who own and till their own farms . . . the men who went to war . . . and saved the nation's honor . . . *by the natural law of their being* find their place in the Republican Party. While the old slave owner and slave driver, the saloon keeper, the ballot box stuffer . . . the criminal class of the great cities, the men who cannot read or write, *by the natural law of their being* find their congenial place in the Democratic Party.

A Massachusetts Senator (Republican) named George F. Hoar arrived at that triumphantly self-satisfied formula toward the end of the 19th century. The delineation suggests what political parties used to be in the U.S. The labels were, for one thing, descriptive: a man who called himself a Democrat embraced impulses, assumptions, leaders and even a cul-

[5] Reprint of magazine article by Lance Morrow, staff writer. *Time.* 112:42. N. 20, '78. Reprinted by permission from TIME, The Weekly Newsmagazine; Copyright Time Inc. 1978.

ture very different from those of the man who called himself a Republican. The political parties functioned in a sense like secular churches, with doctrines and powers of intercession, with saints, rites, duties, disciplines and rewards. From wards to White House, the parties were crucial to the way the country worked. The old Tammany boss Carmine De Sapio remembered hauling coal as a young party errand boy to keep families of voters from freezing in the winter. A millionaire political boss like Mark Hanna could install William McKinley as President.

Today the parties have virtually collapsed as a force in American politics. This fall's campaigns were emphatic confirmation of a trend that has been at work for a decade or more: the draining of energy and resources away from the parties and into a sort of fragmented political free-for-all. The extent of the political transformation can be seen in the extravagant use of television, which more than any other single factor has cut loose candidates from their parties and allowed them to inject themselves directly into the constituent consciousness: individual packaging instead of bulk. In this election, TV spending by candidates for Congress and state offices exceeded anything in the past.

Ask any American today to list five words with which he would describe himself. It is rare that Republican or Democrat will be on the list. In fact, a sizable number of candidates in this fall's campaign displayed an amazing reticence about letting the voters know what their party was; the affiliation was widely regarded as either an encumbrance or an irrelevance. In New Jersey, a voter reading one key piece of Senatorial Candidate Jeffrey Bell's literature could not have told whether he was running as a Republican or a Rosicrucian.

House Speaker "Tip" O'Neill surveyed the party's centrifugal forces last week and remarked: "If this were France, the Democratic Party would be five parties." The somewhat chaotic individualism of American politics these days can have its charm, but it is also dangerous. Congress now has all the discipline of a five-year-old's birthday party. Toby Moffett, 34, a Democratic Connecticut Congressman who was not

even a member of the party until a couple of weeks before he
filed in 1974, remarks with some chagrin: "We get to Washington and we're not prone to look for leadership the way
they used to. We don't owe anybody anything." With several
hundred different ideas caroming around the Capitol about
how to handle energy or inflation, it is difficult to make policy. It is also much harder for the man in the White House to
use party discipline to bring Congressmen into line behind his
program. Jimmy Carter, who for the first two years of his
term incautiously neglected relations with the national Democratic Party, found that he could not attack from the cul-
prit's rear, by way of the party structure back home.

The decline of the parties is part of the atomizing process
of American culture. "The individualistic instincts in this society," writes Washington *Post* Columnist David Broder,
"have now become much more powerful in our politics than
the majoritarian impulse. It is easier and more appealing for
all of us—leaders as well as followers—to separate ourselves
from the mass than to seek out the alliances that can make us
part of a majority." Voters seem to have lost the psychological need to feel themselves part of a large political cause; the
Viet Nam War, Watergate and other scandals have left a
deep residual cynicism that instructs Americans to beware of
politicians.

Many other conditions have helped to reduce the parties'
circumstances. The relentless attention of pollsters to the
public mood means that candidates and officeholders receive
their instructions directly from the people, rather than
through the party apparatus. Impresarios of media—like
White House Adviser Gerald Rafshoon—orchestrate campaigns without the party's help or intervention. The very reforms that the parties instituted to purify the system (the
proliferation of primaries, the funding of campaigns by political action groups instead of the old fat cats) have helped to
destroy it. Says Joel Fleishman, director of Duke University's
Institute for Policy Sciences: "With laudable motives, we've
actually contributed to the degeneration of the political
process."

The traditional party structures served to organize possibilities, to discipline people and ideas into workable forms. When practically every politician is a free agent, there is a tendency toward the anarchic, which may be a perfect political reflection of a narcissistic decade. In the absence of party loyalty, officeholders may find it easier to exercise their integrity, although of course they may also owe fealty to some private lobby. In either case, they tend to lose the talent for compromise and concerted effort. Single-issue zealotry, which is rewarded in the new enlarged primary system, can contaminate the entire political process.

Announcements of the death of the two-party system are issued regularly, of course, usually just befor the two-party system reasserts itself with a certain amount of resilience. "Everything is cyclical," remarks Stanley Friedman, the Bronx County Democratic chairman in New York. "It used to be fashionable to beat the bosses. Now people are recognizing that you can get strong leadership from an organized political establishment." Still, it is clear that the powers and purposes of both parties are becoming thoroughly circumscribed. It would be lamentable if some day the nation's two great political parties were reduced to performing merely decorative and ceremonial duties, with candidates taking the party label in the same spirit that ships sail under Liberian registry—a flag of convenience, and no more.

REPUBLICAN RENAISSANCE[6]

The death of the Republican party is hardly a new story in American politics. Obituaries for the GOP were written in 1964, following the Goldwater debacle; in 1974, following Richard Nixon's resignation and the GOP's disastrous midterm election losses and, in 1976, after the Reagan-Ford split

[6] Excerpted from magazine article by Alan Baron, Washington editor, *Politics Today*. *Politics Today*. 6:26–8+. Ja.–F. '79. © 1979 by Politics Today, Inc. All rights reserved.

at the GOP convention and Jimmy Carter's November
victory.

The trendlines for the party are certainly not good. In
1944, at the time of Franklin Roosevelt's fourth election to
the presidency, the Gallup Poll reported that Americans were
about evenly divided between the parties: 41 percent called
themselves Democrats and 39 percent labeled themselves Republicans. Today, the Democratic figure is up, slightly, to
about 44 percent. But the GOP has fallen to 22 percent. (Independents make up the difference.)

Republicans have fallen behind the Democrats in every
region in the country, including such traditional GOP strong-
holds as New England and the plains states. Democrats also
outnumber Republicans in every segment of the electorate,
including, surprisingly, business and professional people,
upper-income people, the college-educated and suburbanites.
In many areas of the country, the proportion of Republicans
among newly registered voters is down to less than 15 percent. And the party has not controlled either house of the
Congress for almost a quarter century—since 1954. Whether
the 1978 elections produced a clear enough change in Republican fortunes to put an end to such talk is unclear. But
they did produce enough victories to put such rhetoric on ice,
at least for a while. The newspapers and networks reported
that the Republicans made "modest" gains. . . .

Just what is the future of the Republican party? To understand that, you've got to first look at what's happening to
the party system in America. In the last few decades, both political parties have become less relevant forces in electoral
politics and all levels of government.

America has never had political parties in the European
sense of the word. Our parties weren't formed to promote a
basic ideology, and party loyalty has never been at a pre-
mium. But parties were essential vehicles for individuals to
gain economic and political power. Prior to the New Deal,
parties were sometimes even the source of direct social benefits: Thanksgiving turkeys for the poor and legal advice for
the immigrant. Party clubs provided a way for ambitious

young men to build law practices or find patronage jobs. And, for a handful, party service led to public office.

Since Social Security, civil service and television, that has changed. Parties no longer do social work; patronage has almost disappeared. Party conventions have been replaced by primaries in which anyone can run, regardless of party support, who has the resources to wage a campaign. Finally, voters no longer need the party to inform them about the campaign or define the issues. They can get that information directly, from the candidates, via television and direct mail.

Thus, split-ticket voting has become the rule rather than the exception, even in the once solidly Democratic south. This year, New Yorkers elected Democrats from New York City as governor, lieutenant governor and attorney general, and voted for an upstate Republican for controller. In California, voters elected a Democratic governor by a near record margin; a Republican lieutenant governor; a Democratic state treasurer; a Republican attorney general and a Democratic state controller. Iowans replaced a liberal Democratic senator with a new right Republican, then replaced a new right Republican attorney general with a liberal Democrat. In Nebraska, voters switched from a Democratic to a Republican governor—and from a Republican to a Democratic senator. In New Hampshire, they did precisely the opposite. Overall, 25 of the 50 states divide their two US Senate seats between the parties; a total of 34 states divide Senate seats and the governorship between the parties. And most of the remaining 16 states aren't one-party bastions, either.

The decline in party loyalty and clout in American politics has been accompanied by another change: the increase in the importance of ideology and issues. As the voters have become better educated and more willing to cross party lines, they've become more influenced by differences between the candidates on specific issues. And, as the number of persons who get into politics for personal economic gain has declined, the relative strength of those who enter it to influence and change public policy has increased. Thus, as the parties have become less important, they have also become more ideological.

The 1978 elections are a good case in point. There were 69 statewide races for senator and governor. In 64 of them, the Democratic candidate was clearly the more liberal one in the race. When the Republicans nominated liberals (e.g., Sen. Ed Brooke in Massachusetts), the Democrats were usually more liberal (e.g., Senator-elect Paul Tsongas); when the Democrats nominated conservatives (e.g., Governor James Exon in Nebraska), the Republicans were even more conservative. There were a few notable exceptions, of course, but that rule has applied in more than 80 percent of the statewide races during the past several elections.

Within the party organizations, the ideological differences are even clearer. The Democratic party has moved to the left; even in such states as Texas and Alabama, liberals control the state party. The Republican party, on the other hand, has moved to the right; even in a liberal state like Massachusetts, Reagan Republicans control the party organization. The differences inside the parties, in fact, are no longer between liberals and conservatives. Rather, they are between ideologues, who are primarily committed to issues, and pragmatists, whose first concern is winning elections.

The important development within the Republican party in 1978 has been the rise of the pragmatists. More than at any time in recent years, the GOP is in a mood to put ideological differences behind it—and unite to win elections.

This changing attitude does not stem from any internal organizational strategy or technique—although GOP Chairman Bill Brock has done a top-notch job. Rather, it reflects changes in the nature of American politics in the last few years, which have affected both parties. These changes stem from a lessening of the bitter and divisive conflicts that shaped our politics in the 1960s and early 1970s.

The first involved race. The civil rights movement's impact on politics was mainly felt in the Democratic party which, with a great deal of pain and under much pressure, allowed black Americans in and invited Dixiecrat segregationists out. What was less noticed was what happened when these segregationists took over the shells of the Republican parties (which until then had barely existed) in the South. The segregationists became a potent force in the GOP—and an inviting source of votes for ambitious Republican politicians. But as these politicians wooed them, they alienated other Republicans, i.e., Republicans who prided themselves on being in the party of Lincoln and Teddy Roosevelt; Republicans from the Midwest and New England who had, for generations, looked with scorn on Dixiecrats and segregationists: Republicans who supported the NAACP and Urban League and whose Congregational ministers and Episcopalian priests marched in Birmingham and Selma. When Barry Goldwater voted against the Civil Rights Act and won the Republican presidential nomination, these Republicans said "enough."

Now race has faded as an issue and the realities of black political clout in the South have forced southern Republicans to change. And Republican efforts to woo the black vote, led by GOP Chairman Brock, have served as notice to those northern "Lincoln Republicans" that "you can come home now."

The second conflict of the 1960s centered on the war in Vietnam. Republicans have usually been for a strong national defense, but they have also opposed foreign intervention. There was strong Republican opposition to participation in the League of Nations and World War II. And there was strong grass-roots Republican antipathy to the Vietnam War. Again, while the battle over Vietnam was mainly seen to be within the Democratic party, it was also taking place within the GOP.

The Republican party still remains split on foreign policy; there was no unanimity on the Panama Canal treaties and there is unlikely to be much on SALT. But neither of these issues evokes quite the passion of Vietnam—and neither is an ongoing issue. (Even the most vehement critics of the Panama treaty agree the issue has pretty much run its course.) Luckily for the GOP, the tension between isolationist and interventionist wings has subsided, for now.

The third conflict involved social issues, the "life-style" issues—abortion, drugs, gay rights, etc.—and "law and order." To some Republicans they are genuine concerns; the Republican party does best among older Americans committed to traditional values, and opposition to change is greatest among them. But to many Republican politicians, these issues have represented a handle for broadening the GOP's base—for reaching out to Catholic, ethnic, blue-collar, conservative Democrats. That's the real reason why a higher proportion of Protestant Republican congressmen oppose abortion than do Catholic Democratic congressmen.

But the gains the GOP made with its hard-line strategy on the social issues were lost, to some extent, in its traditional base, upper-middle-income, suburban Protestants. The loss was sharpest among young college-educated people from high socioeconomic backgrounds. In 1956, this group voted 60 percent Republican in races for Congress. In 1968, it split evenly. By 1976, it was voting 65 percent Democratic. Spiro Agnew's rhetoric and Richard Nixon's Watergate had, noted consultant Mark Shields, "cost the Republicans a whole generation of potential leaders."

Those young people who remained in the Republican fold were, most often, ideological conservatives. Many of them were "libertarians" who opposed government interference in any sphere of private life. While they didn't always approve of the life-style of the liberal campus activists, they did defend their rights. And now many of these libertarians are serving as speech writers and campaign planners and even candidates for the GOP. Their views are having an impact; they've moved the GOP to a bit more liberal—or at least more libertarian—attitude on social issues, one that is now not far from that of most Americans.

As race, war and life-styles have faded as cutting issues, economics has returned. And economics is not a bitterly divisive issue within the GOP.

There are differences, to be sure. But even the most liberal Republicans are more conservative than moderately liberal Democrats, like President Carter, on national health insurance. And there's virtually across-the-board unanimity among Republicans that the way to boost the economy is by cutting government spending and providing tax breaks for business for capital investment. Individual Republicans adjust their views to their particular constituencies, but economic issues do not tear the party apart.

TWO-PARTY POLITICS IN THE SOUTH[7]

An interesting fact about the 1976 election went virtually unnoticed, namely, that for the first time since the Civil War, southern whites voted the same way for president as did whites outside the South. According to a CBS News/*New York Times* poll of presidential voters taken on election day 1976, both southern and nonsouthern whites gave a slight majority to Gerald Ford—52 percent for Ford and 48 percent for Carter. Carter won by an overwhelming margin—as much as ten to one—among black voters nationwide. But blacks had given almost as much support to George McGovern in 1972, who won barely one-third of the white vote nationwide. Jimmy Carter's accomplishment was to bring so many whites, and particularly so many southern whites, back to the Democratic party.

The election of the first president from the Deep South since Zachary Taylor was the culmination of a long series of developments. Political trends since World War II have been in the direction of reintegrating the South with the rest of the nation. This may seen strange, given the fact that the most wrenching and protracted political conflict of the past 25 years, the civil rights revolution, divided North and South more deeply than at any time since the Civil War. But the fact is that the civil rights movement has liberated the South

[7] Reprint of magazine article "Welcome Back: With the Discovery of Two-Party Politics, the South Has Finally Rejoined the Union," by William Schneider, contributing editor, *Politics Today*. *Politics Today*. 6:58-9. Ja.-F. '79. © 1979 by Politics Today, Inc. All rights reserved.

from its obsession with race. Jimmy Carter has said many times, quite correctly, that neither he nor any other white southerner could ever have been elected president were it not for Martin Luther King and the civil rights movement.

The most direct evidence of the convergence of North and South comes from poll data on racial attitudes. The Gallup poll asked white parents in 1963, 1973 and 1978 whether they would object to sending their children to a school in which (a) there were a *few* black students, (b) about *half* the students were black, and (c) *more than half* the students were black. In 1963, only 10 percent of northern whites objected to sending their children to a school where there were a few black students, while 61 percent of southern whites wanted total segregation. In 1978, a mere 5 percent of northern whites favored totally segregated schools. But the decline of segregationist sentiment among southern whites over this 15-year period was trule remarkable; by 1978, only 7 percent of southern whites said that they would object to sending their children to schools in which there were a few black students.

White parents objected more strongly to sending their children to schools that were half-black, but still the trend was in the liberal direction. Objections among northern whites to a school that was half-black fell from 33 percent in 1963 to 23 percent in 1978, while objections among southern whites fell from 78 to 28 percent. In other words, northern and southern whites had been 45 percentage points apart on this question in 1963. By 1978, the regional difference had fallen to only 5 percent.

The degree of regional polarization also declined in the case of Gallup's third question, whether parents would object to sending their children to a school that was more than half-black. But the trendlines in this case show a revealing, if temporary, twist. Southern white objections to majority black schools fell from 86 percent in 1963 to 69 percent in 1973. But the number of northern white parents who objected to sending their children to majority black schools actually increased, from 53 percent in 1963 to 63 percent in 1973. This countertendency to the dominant trend toward liberalization was very likely a reaction to busing, which began in 1970.

But by 1978, opposition to majority black schools had declined to less than a majority of white parents in both the North and the South. This year, 39 percent of northern white parents and 49 percent of southern white parents said they had an objection to sending their children to such schools. Thus the inexorable liberalization of racial attitudes appears to have overcome even the antibusing reaction.

In 1963, southern whites averaged 43 percent more anti-integration than northern whites on these three questions, with the largest difference occurring on the most basic issue of segregation—whether white children should go to schools with even a few black children. Now, the difference between northern and southern whites averages just 6 percent, with almost no disagreement on the basic issue of segragation.

The civil rights revolution has also liberated the South from the one-party system, a fact that has brought southern politics in line with the rest of the nation. To understand what has happened, one must first understand that all of southern political history has been an interplay between two conflicts—race and class.

The antebellum party system in the South reflected a rural class division. The Whig party represented the wealthier merchants, planters and slaveowners, while the Jacksonian Democrats drew strong support from the poorer class of white farmers in the "up-country" where there were few plantations and few slaves. This regional division in southern politics has persisted to the present day, the "conservative" whites in the heavily black plantation counties against the "radical" whites who work the small, hardscrabble farms of the predominantly white areas.

The Civil War eliminated the Whigs and established the Republicans as the party of unionism, abolition, and, later, carpetbaggery and Negro rule. The conservative southern planters, who had been the strongest supporters of secession and war, latched on to the Democratic party and used it as an instrument to unite southern whites and "redeem" the South from the horrors of Reconstruction. The Democrats became the conservative party of the South, and so they remained until the civil rights revolution of the present era.

Blacks were caught between the two great contending forces. Populists tried to appeal to the black vote, often with considerable success, on the basis of a common class interest. Conservative Democrats, on the other hand, were the ruling elite in the areas where most blacks lived. Conservatives tended to have moderate and paternalistic racial attitudes, in contrast to the Negrophobia that was rampant among poorer whites. Conservatives often controlled the black vote through a combination of local influence and, where "necessary," intimidation and outright fraud.

Conservatives panicked at the onslaught of populism in the 1890s. Fearful of a very real revolutionary threat, they did what skillful politicians always try to do when the odds are against them—they shifted the focus of conflict, in this case, from class to race. They raised the cry of white supremacy and unleashed the forces of virulent race hatred. The result was that the late nineteenth century witnessed the worst outburst of racial violence in all of southern history.

The solution proposed by the conservatives was to remove the Negro completely from political life and to codify a system of total racial segregation—Jim Crow. The effect of the disfranchisement movement, in which blacks in every southern state lost all political rights between 1890 and 1910, was to eliminate class, not race, from southern politics. Why was this the case?

The conservatives created the solid South, whose crowning institution was the one-party state. Whites of all classes closed ranks around the Democratic party, which became, first and foremost, the party of white supremacy. Any challenge to the Democratic party was, by definition, a challenge to white supremacy and so raised the threat of "Negro rule" and race mixing. Instead of eliminating race from southern politics, eliminating the Negro eliminated everything *but* race from southern politics, at least in terms of partisan conflict.

In the solid South, economic conflict shifted from party politics to the Democratic primaries. Contests between economic radicals and conservatives did occur, but within a restricted white electorate and among candidates who could not be differentiated by party.

What the civil rights revolution accomplished, of course, is the reenfranchisement of blacks and the dismantling of the Jim Crow system. In 1960, 61 percent of whites and 29 percent of blacks were registered to vote in the 11 states of the old Confederacy. The black registration rate in Mississippi was a scandalous 5 percent. By 1976, as a result of the Voting Rights Act of 1965 and the organized efforts of voter education projects, the registration rate among southern blacks had risen to 63 percent, almost equal to the 68 percent of southern whites registered to vote. In Mississippi, the black registration rate was no less than 61 percent.

The civil rights revolution—aptly called by some "the second Reconstruction"—accomplished what no internal opposition could ever do in the South: it used the federal government, an outside force, to challenge and destroy the edifice of white supremacy. Despite the efforts of officials such as Faubus and Wallace to keep the issue of white supremacy alive, most southern voters quickly realized that segregation was no longer a viable option. Reenfranchising southern blacks has not had the effect of subordinating all politics to the race issue, any more than disfranchising blacks 88 years ago eliminated the race issue. The effect has actually been to reduce racial polarization and to create the basis for real class politics in the South for the first time in over 100 years.

The Republican party has begun to assume its logical role as the organized expression of Southern economic conservatism—the role that the Republicans have played on the national level since before the New Deal. The pattern of the 1976 presidential vote in the South is revealing. The Republican candidate carried the middle- and upper-middle-class white vote in suburbs and metropolitan areas, while the Democrat piled up large margins in poorer urban and rural areas, as well as among blacks. This same class difference has become common in statewide partisan contests as racial antagonism has declined.

The Republican party in the South has been built from the top down. Republicans have been most competitive with Democrats in presidential voting and have done increasingly well in statewide elections. The party has done least well at the local level, where the conservative Democratic tradition still holds sway in many areas. In the 1950s, the Republican proportion of the southern congressional delegation was virtually constant at 7 percent. Since 1968, Republicans have consistently won at least a quarter of the House seats in the South, a figure that rose to 29 percent this year.

The party now holds three southern governorships, including a major breakthrough in Texas, which has just elected its first Republican governor since 1874. The southern contests for the US Senate were especially significant in 1978. Every one of the five southern Republican Senate seats was at stake (North Carolina, South Carolina, Virginia, Texas, Tennessee). All of these senators had been elected or reelected in 1972, when it could be argued that the peculiar circumstances of the Nixon-McGovern contest exaggerated Republican support in the South. Nevertheless, the Republicans held on to all five seats in 1978 and even added a new Republican senator from Mississippi.

Meanwhile, Jimmy Carter represents the new face of the Democratic party in the South, an economically progressive coalition of blacks and poorer whites. The "New South" Democrats have done best in those southern states with the strongest populist traditions—most notably, Georgia and Arkansas. Republicans, on the other hand, have made their greatest gains in areas where "Bourbon" Democrats long predominated. Virginia, the southern state with the weakest populist tradition, has elected three Republican governors in a row. Virginians have not elected a Democrat to the Senate since 1966 and now have a Republican majority in their congressional delegation. Virginia was also the only southern state carried by Ford in 1976.

All these developments point to the gradual rationalization of southern politics. Indeed, the emergence of truly competitive politics in the South along lines of economic interest, long buried beneath the obsession with race, is one of the few unambiguously positive trends in American politics today.

THE TWO-PARTY SYSTEM— UNIQUE AND LASTING[8]

Reprinted from *U.S. News & World Report*

Since elections are won by numbers, the primary task of any party is to attract as many voters as possible. Traditionally, this means building the party, Republican or Democratic, around the broadest possible political philosophy.

The party's program for change, or "platform," must appeal to many segments of voters—businessmen, farmers, laborers, ethnic minorities and others—if the party hopes to compete seriously for the Presidency.

This has led to accusations that, as Alabama Governor Wallace often said, there is "not a dime's worth of difference" between the two parties. However, political experts who have examined party platforms say that while the distinctions often are vague, they are significant.

The Republicans generally embrace a more conservative political philosophy than the Democrats. For instance, the 1976 GOP platform stressed the need for reduced federal spending, more local control and less government interference in the economy. The Democrats, meanwhile, emphasized greater use of the government's powers to promote full employment, relieve poverty and enforce civil-rights laws.

While both parties depend mainly on their moderate majorities for direction, both have liberal and conservative wings that can exert influence on specific issues. Internal debate

[8] Excerpted from staff-written magazine article. *U.S. News & World Report.* 85:39–41. S. 18, '78.

over programs and candidates can be—and often is—
spirited. . . .

Steady Gains for Women and Minorities

Women and members of minority groups are gaining
steadily if slowly in political influence both as voters and as
candidates.

Operating inside and outside the two major parties, these
alliances are making their presence felt from town councils to
the White House. Evidence of progress—and the distance left
to go—is clear from recent reports.

Although women have had the vote nationwide since
1920, their impact in politics has not been in proportion to
their percentage of the population. The number of female
state legislators has doubled to 702 in the last 10 years, but
that still is only 9 percent of the total. Women comprise 51.3
percent of the nation's population and 52.2 percent of persons
of voting age, but they hold only about 8 percent of elective
offices. In 1978, only 20 of 535 members of Congress were
women. At the same time, the nation had only two female
governors and three lieutenant governors.

Political experts note that more female candidates are
seeking and winning local and state offices, and predict that
as women gain experience their numbers and influence in national posts will increase rapidly.

Inside the major parties, women are winning a growing
but as yet still unequal voice. In 1968, women made up 13
percent of delegates to the Democratic national convention.
Rule reforms expanded that share to 40 percent in 1972, but
females slipped to 34 percent of the delegates in 1976.
Women held 17 percent of delegate seats at the 1968 Republican national convention. The figure rose to about 30 percent
in 1972 and 1976.

Leaders of women's groups are quick to remind politicians that the turnout of women at the polls has climbed to
the point where it lags only slightly behind that of men. At
the same time, the women's-liberation movement has helped

to form several feminine political groups, some crossing party lines, that are dedicated to increasing the number and effectiveness of women public officials.

Belated surge. Blacks, although theoretically able to vote since 1870, did not hold many elective offices until passage of the Voting Rights Act in 1965. By 1977, the number of blacks elected to public office had risen to 4,311—a jump of 254 percent in a decade. By 1978, there were 16 blacks in the House of Representatives and one in the Senate, and there were two black lieutenant governors. Several major cities—including Los Angeles, Atlanta, Washington, Newark, Detroit and New Orleans—had black mayors. Still, blacks are far from holding office in proportion to their nearly 12 percent share of the U.S. population.

A heavy majority of black votes in national elections in recent years has gone to Democratic candidates. An estimated 90 percent of voting blacks backed Jimmy Carter in 1976. Some authorities, in fact, credit blacks with giving Carter his narrow victory.

Gaining influence within the political parties, however, has been a slower process. Blacks gradually rose to comprise 15 percent of the delegation at the 1972 Democratic National Convention but fell to 11 percent in 1976. They held 4 percent of the Republican National Convention slots in 1968 but slipped to 3 percent in 1976.

Although both parties have special organizations to court them, women and blacks have felt compelled to form bipartisan political arms to make themselves heard. These groups get people to the polls, help finance candidates and lobby for legislation outside the party structures.

Both national conventions in 1976 saw women fight for and win concessions from leaders of their own parties. Women at the Republican convention, threatening a floor fight, won support for the equal-rights amendment in the party platform. Democratic women used similar tactics to persuade Carter to commit himself to a greater emphasis on women's rights. Blacks work through several lobbying groups to pressure both the parties and government agencies.

While not considered as vital today as in previous years, the "ethnic vote" is still important to politicians. Both parties have special staffs to work with groups representing people of Italian, Jewish, Polish, Irish, German, Hispanic and other heritages. No big-city campaign is thought to be complete until a candidate visits an ethnic affair to eat a taco or dance the polka.

Breaking habits. Political lore has it that ethnic groups fall into regular voting habits. The Poles and the Irish are said to generally vote Democratic; the Germans and people of Baltic descent favor the Republicans, and so on. If that ever was true, however, the pattern has been broken in recent years.

Like others, ethnic voters have learned that they can achieve their greatest impact by applying pressure directly to lawmakers and public agencies instead of working through political parties. Their influence is felt often in Washington on such issues as strife in the Mideast, immigration policy and relations with Cuba.

It is the rare politician who dares to ignore the increasingly effective role played by women and minority groups in local, state and national affairs.

The Growing Impact of Independents

The most pivotal—and most courted—American voters today are neither Democrats nor Republicans, but a large and vaguely defined group called independents.

The number of nonaligned voters is growing, having overtaken declared Republicans several years ago and now closing in on those who label themselves Democrats.

The Gallup Poll reports that Americans identifying themselves as independents grew from 16 percent in 1937 to 31 percent in 1977. Those declaring as Republicans dropped in the same period from 34 to 20 percent, and self-labeled Democrats went from 50 to 49 percent.

Why the big increase in nonaffiliated voters? Most experts attribute it to the decline of big-city political machines as urban residents have headed for the suburbs. The progressively complex nature of campaign issues and higher education levels could be other factors.

Because of their very nature, independent voters are not subject to being charted in the usual profiles. Analysts report, however, that the group consists primarily of two segments of the nation's population that are almost diametrically opposed.

One big faction is made up of the politically disinterested—those who seldom go to the polls, the less educated and workers who do not belong to a labor organization.

The other group consists of better-educated voters, who are quite likely to cast ballots but don't care for partisan politics and who "vote the man" or an issue espoused by the candidate. These are the ticket splitters. They may vote for a Republican for President and a Democrat for the Senate, or vice versa, in the same election.

The independent also tends to be a middle-of-the-roader. With some geographical exceptions, most voters who pledge allegiance to one of the two major parties tend to do so out of a firm belief in a party's political philosophy.

Result: The independent has become a major target in all statewide and national campaigns. The prime efforts by both organized parties are to get their own voters to the polls and then to swing enough independents to win the election. Political advertising, particularly television commercials, is aimed primarily at the independent voter, who is presumably late in making up his mind.

Since Republican candidates for the Presidency have captured as much as 61 percent of the total vote in recent elections and have not fallen below 37 percent since 1936, it is clear that the GOP hasa been more successful in wooing independents in national elections. However, enough independents have tended to support Democrats in congressional elections to keep them in control.

Independents on the ballot. Political candidates occasionally seek election under an independent banner. Maine elected an independent as governor in 1974, when James

Longley won a three-way race with only 39 percent of the total vote. But even in this case, Longley had been a registered Democrat, and renounced his party affiliation not long before making his decision to run.

Senator Harry F. Byrd, Jr., of Virginia technically has run twice as an independent and won. However, he caucuses with Democrats in the Senate and receives his committee assignments from the Democratic Party.

Independents as candidates do not figure to be much of a factor. But the voter who refuses to be identified with either major party increasingly is turning out to be a decisive force in the American electoral process.

"LAST HURRAH" FOR
OLD-TIME POLITICS?[9]
Reprinted from *U.S. News & World Report*

Politicians in the next decade will be confronted with a new breed of voters—angry, unpredictable and, yet, politically apathetic.

Voters, in turn, will force shifts in political campaigning:

☐ Candidates, relying less and less on their parties, will concentrate on building their own coalitions. Parties will continue losing influence.

☐ Minorities and special interests will swing more elections.

☐ The first billion-dollar election year is approaching, giving a boost to the idea of public financing of elections below the presidential level.

☐ Advertising, computers and highly paid consultants will dominate more and more political contests.

---

[9] Excerpted from staff-written magazine article. *U.S. News & World Report*. 87:70-1. O. 15, '79.

☐ Tax saving will spread as an issue, possibly enabling local governments and officials to gain power.

The 1980s, in short, will force old-style politicians and public officials to change in many ways.

As one analyst puts it: "Politicians are going to be looking at larger numbers of voters who are growing older, are moving south, are more turned off and are fiercely independent when they even bother to cast their ballots."

Demographics will be important. Migration and other population shifts will transfer more power to the sun belt after the 1980 census. California, Texas and Florida figure to be the big gainers in seats in the House of Representatives, while New York, Ohio and Illinois are likely to be among the main losers.

The electorate will age. The number of citizens 65 and over will jump from 24.9 million in 1980 to 29.8 million in 1990. The percentage of elderly voters in the overall population will go from 15.5 to 16.7 percent in the decade.

If past performance is any guide, most older voters will be conservative, especially on issues of taxes and government spending. All indications are that they also will be more tightly organized to protect their interests on matters such as pensions, medical insurance and housing.

Aside from special interests, public apathy will be a problem for politicians of the 1980s. The source of the voter disinterest is traced by public-opinion polls showing that growing numbers of citizens have little confidence in the Presidency, Congress and political parties. The judiciary also is losing ground. Most experts doubt that this pattern of lingering distrust, fueled by revelations in the Vietnam era and Watergate scandals, can be reversed in the next 10 years.

Many analysts also are skeptical that political parties will be able to regain much, if any, of the influence they have lost recently. A Gallup Poll indicates that the proportion of voters who regard themselves as independents has increased from one fourth to one third since 1970.

Experts blame the decline of political parties on efforts to open them up to broader public participation and to reduce the power of a handful of leaders. The unintended result, some analysts say, is that experienced politicians increasingly are being shouldered aside by newcomers who have the ability to wage and win popular campaigns, but who may, after gaining election, lack either the experience or the constituency needed to perform their duties.

Jeane J. Kirkpatrick, a Georgetown University political-science professor, says of the party fracturing: "The process of decomposition has affected both state and national parties, their organizations and their rank and file."

Promising to add to the uncertainty of future elections is the escalating number of presidential primaries, which has jumped from 15 in 1968 to as many as 36 in 1980, as state legislatures grab the chance to gain notice. Some political scientists are concerned that the primary system, designed to take power from party bosses at the nominating conventions, has only transferred it to patchwork bands of activists that can swing a certain primary, but that have little continuity or broad philosophy.

Special-interest power. Experts speculate that politicians, unable to rely any longer on party discipline, will concentrate increasingly on building their own power bases. Future candidates of both parties are expected to seek combinations of often-disparate coalitions from among organized pressure groups—without regard to party labels or loyalties.

Office seekers also will be forced in the decade ahead to deal with a growing number of movements focused on one cause. Some of these single-issue groups, such as anti-abortion and consumer forces, are working for recognition as separate political parties, as well as pressuring candidates to stand with them.

Minorities are shaping up as another formidable political force.

Blacks, who accounted for about 7.5 million votes in the 1976 election, say the Democratic Party has taken them too much for granted in the past and promise to be more independent in future elections. Hispanics, members of the fastest growing minority group in the country, already boast significant numbers in the key electoral states of New York, California, Texas and Florida—and warn that they will be demanding more from future candidates who want their votes.

In the next decade, women's groups will be out to better their record of the last five years, in which their number in public office has doubled.

Running for office promises to grow even more expensive and media oriented than it is today. The money spent on elective and party politics at all levels in 1980 is expected to top 700 million dollars, so the nation's first billion-dollar election year may not be far off.

Inflation alone will boost the cost of running for office. As much as 50 percent of future campaign budgets is expected to go for television advertising, a key element in the "packaging" of today's candidates.

Public dollars. With taxpayers already paying most costs of presidential campaigning, special interests can be counted on to step up efforts to influence the outcome of Senate and House contests through political-action committees. Controversy over those efforts is certain to trigger renewed attempts in the 1980s to obtain public financing for congressional races.

Analysts predict that the personalized style of political campaigning, tailored expressly for television, will become even more popular. The highly paid campaign consultant, or image maker, will play a bigger role in national and statewide races.

Increasingly, computers will be used to analyze public moods, single out hot issues, target voters and raise money through massive direct-mail appeals. The Republican National Committee in Washington already has 22 employes operating two computers linked to state party organizations. The Democrats, playing catch up, say they have the start of a good system.

The struggle for power and taxing authority between Washington, the 50 state capitals and the nation's urban centers shows no sign of letup in the decade ahead. Tax-cutting fever ignited by the adoption of Proposition 13 last year in

California is still catching in many states and is likely to continue at least into the early 1980s.

More states' rights. Some analysts see a possibility that public disenchantment with the federal bureaucracy will enable state and local governments to regain some of their lost power as voters try to settle problems closer to home.

But whether they are handled in Washington or at city hall, taxes, inflation and government regulation are seen as the dominant political issues of the next 10 years, just as they have been for most of this decade.

The big difference: Mingled fury and disenchantment on the part of voters and continuing fragmentation of the traditional electoral process promise to make politics in the 1980s a tougher game than ever before.

EDITOR'S INTRODUCTION

The declining fortunes of the two major parties would seem to be the occasion for other parties to step in and seize some of the power they have lost. This has not happened for several reasons.

Finding adequate financing is a major problem for minor parties. Fund-raising legislation, limiting individual contributions to political candidates, makes money scarce for third-party candidates, who lack an initial broad base of support. (Third parties have for the most part functioned on local and state levels—for example, the Farmer-Labor Party in Minnesota and the Conservative Party in New York State.) Another problem has been the lack of dynamic leadership. In the past, national third-party movements rallied around a colorful or strong leader such as Theodore Roosevelt (the Bull Moose Party), Norman Thomas (the Socialist Party) or George Wallace (the American Independent Party). This kind of leadership is not in evidence today.

Many of those who in the past might have provided support for a third party are now operating within the two-party system. Rhodes Cook, in an excerpt from the *Congressional Quarterly Weekly Report*, states that ever since George Wallace deserted the American Independent Party and returned to the Democratic fold, the role of a third party as a vehicle of protest has been weakened. Shut out of the national press and chronically short of funds, Cook says, most third parties, with the possible exception of the Libertarian Party, are withering. The article that follows is a *Newsweek* report on the Libertarian Party and on an even newer group, the Citizens Party.

The Libertarian Party, which advocates the theory of minimum government and espouses laissez-faire policies on most issues, is also the subject of the next selection, a news story by Gladwin Hill, of the New York *Times* staff. The Libertarian candidate for President garnered 171,627 votes in the 1976 presidential election and the Libertarians have, of late, been the most successful of the minor-party devotees. Almost one third of the party's following consists of college students.

Richard J. Margolis, writing for the *New Leader*, records the recent birth of the Citizens Party, "a gleam in the eye of Barry Commoner and his sun-struck minions," who represent "the New Improved Left." Environmentalists and decentralists, they see democracy threatened by big government and big business.

The Democratic Socialist Organizing Committee (D.S.O.C.), according to Harold Meyerson, a Los Angeles-based writer and member of the D.S.O.C. national board, was formed out of the antiwar minority of the old Socialist Party. Writing in the *Nation*, Meyerson depicts the D.S.O.C. as "radicals on a tightrope," believers in socialist ideas who are working within the Democratic Party in order to remain within the mainstream of American politics.

The D.S.O.C.'s counterpart at the other end of the political spectrum is the New Right (not to be confused with the Neoconservatives, who are, for the most part, reformed Liberals). A *Time* account surveys the ultraconservative, activist New Right as it continues to do battle against those who oppose its goals—"a drastic reduction in government and a hard anti-Communist line abroad."

The last article in this section discusses the neoconservative movement. Professor Karl O'Lessker, senior editor of the *American Spectator*, finds neoconservatism—"a set of highly prudential approaches to policy that include most particularly a deep skepticism about the ability of big government to accomplish very much"—the next best hope of the Republican Party in its search for a philosophical tool with which to beat back the Democrats, whose orthodox liberalism is perceived to be in a state of intellectual exhaustion.

THIRD PARTIES ARE WEAKER THAN EVER[1]

While America's two major parties steadily decline in influence, minor parties are quietly declining with them, failing to take advantage of the historical tendency for such groups to exploit voter frustration with the existing political system.

Badly underfinanced for the most part and starving for media attention, third party candidates will not garner enough votes this year even to influence the outcome of many elections.

"The organized third party structure is very weak," observes conservative direct mail specialist Richard Viguerie. "They lack leadership. Third parties usually succeed because they are built around a strong personality. Universally they lack that now."

Viguerie flirted briefly in 1976 with the idea of joining the American Independent Party, a remnant of George Wallace's 1968 presidential campaign, but he sees little value now in joining a third party. Federal legislation limiting the ability of third parties to raise money in presidential elections, and state statutes restricting ballot access, have made it extremely difficult for third parties to develop as national forces. "The laws," Viguerie says, "make it incredibly difficult to work within third parties. It makes all the sense in the world for conservatives to work within the major party framework." [For a profile of Richard Viguerie, see "King Midas of 'The New Right,' " in Section IV, below.]

With an increasing emphasis on operating within the major parties, conservatives are weakening the traditional role of third parties as vehicles of protest. This has shown up this year in the sharp decline from both 1974 and 1976 in the number of third party House candidates. The falloff has been particularly severe for the Wallace remnant parties—which

[1] Excerpted from article by Rhodes Cook, staff writer. *Congressional Quarterly Weekly Report.* 36:3110–12. O. 28, '78. Copyright 1978 Congressional Quarterly Inc. Reprinted by permission.

are listed on the ballot in most states as the American or American Independent Party. Only the fledgling Libertarian Party is running more candidates than it did in 1974.

With his ability to articulate the frustrations of many American voters, Wallace had the opportunity to create one of the most effective third parties in the 20th century. But he chose to use it solely as a vehicle for his presidential candidacy and made only a limited effort to elect his running mates for other offices. Wallace returned to the Democratic Party shortly before the 1972 election, leaving his third party alive but without the recognized leader needed to give it national importance.

The third party route to federal and state office has always been a difficult one, but it has traditionally attracted ideologues who preferred to remain loyal to their own ideological beliefs rather than join a major party.

Before 1950, organized third parties like the Populists, Bull Moosers, and the LaFollette and Wallace Progressives won at least a few U.S. House seats in nearly every election. In the last quarter century, however, there has been no third party with a comparable grass roots base. The few candidates elected to high office without major support, such as Gov. James Longley of Maine, elected in 1974, and Virginia Sen. Harry F. Byrd, Jr., twice returned to the Senate, have chosen to run as independents instead of joining a third party or starting a new one of their own.

In 1976, there were only 15 House elections and two Senate contests in which third-party candidates even drew a share of the vote which exceeded the winner's margin of victory.

Money Problems

All third parties and most independent candidates share a similar problem—money. In the 1976 campaign, when Democrats and Republicans were raising millions of dollars and receiving more than $21 million apiece from the federal government to finance their presidential election campaigns, third parties and independent Eugene J. McCarthy were

scrounging to raise a fraction of this total through private donations. According to a Federal Election Commission report,
only one party, the Communists, were able to collect even
$500,000 for their presidential campaign.

Fund-raising problems are hindering third party and independent challenges again . . . [in 1978]. Mississippi Senate
candidate Charles Evers, the black mayor of Fayette and one
of the most highly publicized of this year's independents, had
been able to raise only $48,800 through the end of September.
His two major party rivals, in contrast, each had collected
more than $600,000.

Money buys attention in the form of media advertising.
Without it, independents and third party candidates are dependent on the press for any publicity that they receive.
Third party spokesmen express satisfaction with the attention
they receive from local media sources, but have been irritated
by the frequent brushoff they have gotten from state and
national media, particularly in their exclusion this year from
televised statewide debates.

The third party effort in a midterm election is also crip-
pled by the absence of a national focus. In a presidential
election, the national ticket provides some cohesion. But in
midterm elections the effort is fragmented and there is less
enthusiasm and money available for ballot access drives.
"Most minor parties," comments former American Independent chairman William Shearer, "do not have strong national
organizations. They are state projects. Whatever is done is
done as a volunteer effort. . . . Whatever the party gets from
me is after a busy day at my law practice."

In recent years most of the successful minor candidates
have been independents rather than third party members. . . .

Carving a Niche

The nation's largest third party, the Libertarians, will not
win any major races . . . [in 1978], but party officials are looking for a higher vote for their candidates than in 1976. "We
want to carve a niche in the wall and build," says Chris

Hocker, the party's national director. "While our candidates were at the 1 to 2 percent level in 1976, we'll be at the 5 to 10 percent level in 1978. The percentage will still be small, but we'll be above the fluke and throw-away vote stage."

The Libertarians, who promote a philosophy of individual responsibility and minimal government interference, are most interested this year in rolling up a large vote in the California governor's race. Although their candidate, Los Angeles attorney Ed Clark, is listed on the ballot as an independent, his advertising clearly identifies him as a Libertarian.

In terms of total number of candidates, the second largest party this year is the Socialist Workers Party. Less ambitious than the Libertarians, they contend their major function is to educate voters, and that they can have as much impact in a strike or demonstration as in an election. "The people who run this country aren't going to let it be changed through elections," declares the party's national director, Bob Schwarz. "And elections, frankly, do not decide policy."

At the beginning of the decade, the remnants of the Wallace third party campaign regularly ran a large number of candidates. But their activity has tapered off. . . .

The American Independent Party is focusing on its slate of candidates in California, and there is some talk that it may decide after the election to retrench.

THIRD PARTIES: POLITICS OF HOPE[2]

The Libertarian Party

Undismayed by the certainty of defeat and unabashedly jumping the gun, the Libertarian Party convened in Los Angeles last week to pick its 1980 Presidential candidate. The 625 delegates overwhelmingly chose Ed Clark, 49, a genial

[2] Reprint of magazine article by Tom Morganthau, associated editor, *Newsweek;* with Martin Kasindorf, Los Angeles bureau; and Frank Maier, Chicago bureau. *Newsweek.* 94:44. S. 17, '79. Copyright 1979, by Newsweek, Inc. All Rights Reserved. Reprinted by Permission.

California antitrust lawyer with the appropriate laissez-faire principles and a political track record that is, by the usual standards, laughable. But four days of speeches and politicking convinced the Libertarians that they are on the verge of becoming a truly national party—and that the conclave itself was the best ever. "This is really big doin's for us," beamed Sherry Watson, 26, of North Carolina. "This party has come of age."

For a party that recorded a mere 5,000 votes in 1972, such roseate optimism seems to border on fantasy—but the Libbies are building. Their 1976 Presidential candidate, Roger Mac-Bride, won 183,187 votes in 32 states, almost 41 million votes behind Jimmy Carter. In 1978, 200 Libertarian candidates for state and local offices rolled up 1.3 million votes and one of them—rugged Alaska insurance man Dick Randolph—was elected to the state legislature, the first Libertarian elected anywhere.

The Libertarians have some big contributors, including Kansas conglomerateur Charles Koch, and their own think tank, the Cato Institute in San Francisco. They believe the time is ripe to crack the Democrat-Republican duopoly in national politics. Their goal next year is to win 2 to 4 per cent of the Presidential vote—a symbolic "balance of power" that Libbies hope will be greater than the margin of victory between the major candidates. "The 1980 campaign," says Randolph, "is primarily a race for public awareness."

Libertarians inhabit an ideological twilight zone where the liberal-conservative dichotomy breaks down. The party's old guard is largely composed of unreconstructed free market-eers who oppose all governmental intervention in the economy. But many younger members are refugees from the New Left whose passion is for individual liberties. The result is a left-right amalgam: Libertarians would abolish social security, oppose reviving the draft, favor a woman's absolute right to abortion and want to eliminate pornography laws. Such logic plays well among the rugged individualists of the Far West, but less happily elsewhere. "In the South, if you talk in terms of the free market, they'll buy it," says delegate Watson. "But the minute you say a person's *body* is his own and you can go to bed with whomever you want, they don't."

Candidate Clark began his political education by supporting then-Republican liberal John Lindsay in New York. "He turned out to be an absolute disaster," Clark says sheepishly. "It was the kind of thing that turned me off to major-party politics." Converted to the Libertarian cause, he ran for governor in California last year against Democrat Jerry Brown and Republican Evelle Younger, and managed to win a respectable 377,960 votes. As the Libertarian standard-bearer, he hopes to be on the Presidential ballot in 40 or more states, peddling free-market solutions for inflation and the energy muddle. With a media-heavy campaign budgeted at up to $4 million, financing could be a problem: party leaders chafe at the $1,000 limit on individual contributions—but reject Federal campaign subsidies on principle. Clark is undeterred. "It is well within the realm of possibility for the Libertarian Party to be the biggest party in the United States" by the 1990s, he says.

The Citizens Party

The Libertarians' confidence in a third-party appeal is mirrored on the left. Now forming for the 1980 election and beyond is the Citizens Party, a coalition of public-interest lobbyists, environmentalists and peace-and-disarmament activists whose heroes are Ralph Nader and ecologist Barry Commoner. The *éminence grise* is Don Rose, a crafty Chicagoan who organized maverick Democrat Jane Byrne's victory over the Daley-Bilandic machine last spring: Rose hopes to launch the party in twenty or more states next year. The party's platform will stress opposition to nuclear power, a greater government role in energy production, guaranteed jobs and stabilized prices.

Clark and Commoner both cite the Republican Party's rapid rise from third-party obscurity as proof of their possibilities, and they share a hearty disdain for the ideological blending they see within the two-party mainstream. Clark hopes to meet his Republican and Democratic rivals in national debate—but if not, he may settle for a joust with the Citizens Party nominee. "At least," suggests one of his supporters, "there would be an intelligent discussion of the issues for a change."

THE LIBERTARIANS[3]

Aiming at the disenchanted, the Libertarian Party chose Ed Clark, an oil company lawyer, last night to run for President in what spokesmen depicted as the 8-year-old party's most auspicious campaign.

The three-day nominating convention was held a year ahead of the major parties' conventions so that members could get on with the difficult job of qualifying the party for the ballot in as many states as possible. The leadership has hopes of qualifying this time in more than 40 states; in two previous national elections, traditional barriers to minority parties forced many Libertarian candidates to run as independents. The convention [was] attended by 600 delegates from all 50 states and the District of Columbia. . . .

The Libertarians, whose candidate received 171,627 votes, or 0.21 percent of the total, in the 1976 Presidential election, consider government essentially a means by which people manipulate and exploit other people. They would abolish most of its apparatus, except for some basic order-keeping functions. [Sources differ slightly on the exact number of votes received.—Ed.]

Large Following in Colleges

The party's faithful include lawyers, philosophers, computer engineers, insurance salesmen and advertising people,

[3] Excerpted from news story "Libertarians, Foes of Big Government, Nominate Coast Lawyer for President," by Gladwin Hill, national correspondent, Los Angeles bureau. New York *Times.* p B 10. S. 10, '79. © 1979 by The New York Times Company. Reprinted by permission.

spanning the ideological spectrum from New Left remnants to the far right of the Liberty League. About one-third of the party's following is on college campuses, and it has a big contingent from the feminist movement.

The common bond is antipathy to big government and what is regarded as its intrusiveness. Folk heroes are mavericks like former Senator Eugene J. McCarthy of Minnesota, Howard Jarvis and Paul Gann, the co-authors of California's tax-cutting Proposition 13, and Nicholas von Hoffman, the columnist, who has said: "For the overtaxed, overburdened and underpowered millions of the American middle class, Libertarians are the only people worth voting for."

The Libertarians' goal is to exert leverage on the major parties and, ultimately, displace them.

Rivals for the Presidential nomination were Mr. Clark, a plain, soft-spoken, 49-year-old lawyer for the Atlantic Richfield Company in Los Angeles, who corralled 377,960 votes as an independent in last year's California gubernatorial context; and Bill Hunscher, a dapper, bearded, 41-year-old computer executive and management consultant from Milford, N.H.

Clash on Need for Convention

The candidates differed chiefly on campaign tactics and a couple of current issues. Mr. Clark favored a national constitutional convention on mandating a balanced Federal budget and the proposed arms-limitation treaty between the United States and the Soviet Union; Mr. Hunscher opposed both.

Mr. Clark won the nomination by a vote of 365 to 195. As his running mate the convention named David Koch, a New York City lawyer who is no relation to the Mayor.

The Libertarian's first Presidential candidate, in 1972, was John Hospers, a University of Southern California philosophy professor, who garnered about 10,000 votes in Washington and Colorado—and one electoral vote from a runaway Nixon elector in Virginia. In 1976, when Mr. McCarthy got 680,390 votes as a third party candidate, the Libertarian nominee,

Roger MacBride, a Virginia lawyer who was the runaway Nixon elector, got 171,627 votes. In the 1978 state and local elections Libertarian candidates amassed over one million votes.

In New York, where the party is known officially as the Free Libertarian Party to avoid confusion with the Liberals, the Libertarian candidate for governor last year, Gray Greenberg, drew 19,000 votes.

The Libertarians see inflation as the big 1980 issue. But they will also begin their campaigning against an array of *bêtes noires.* Their platform perennially lists several dozen major objections to institutions, each likely to strike a responsive chord with one interest group and infuriate another.

They are against the draft and for legalizing marijuana. They are opposed to compulsory public education, anti-gun laws and prosecution of "victimless" crimes.

In the economic realm, they are for classic laissez-faire policies: abolition of tariffs, the Federal Reserve System and the governmental regulation of utilities, and "eventual repeal of all taxation." They would convert public lands to private ownership, end Government controls on water, and abolish the Environmental Protection Agency, leaving pollution to be dealt with through "modified" laws on nuisance and negligence.

Traditional Trappings Dropped

In implicit rejection of "establishment" customs, their assemblage omitted some traditional convention trappings. The convention hall stage was flagless, adorned only with a Libertarian banner. The convention opened with no Pledge of Allegiance, no prayer, no gaveling.... The keynote speaker [was] Roy A. Childs Jr., the 350-pound, black-bearded editor of the *Libertarian Review.*

Invoking the spirit of the American Revolution in a 45-minute stemwinder, he declared: "Our forebears fought and died only to have their visions betrayed. When tyranny is here, submission is a crime!"

THE CITIZENS PARTY[4]

Some of my acquaintances are in political labor again,
hoping to give birth at a national convention next spring to
the Citizens Party. It would be the latest entry in America's
dappled history of third-party pregnancies.

So far the Citizens Party is just a bright idea—a gleam in
the eye of Barry Commoner and his sun-struck minions—but
a sizable and talented organizing committee is already hard
at work, some money from friends and well-wishers is trick-
ling in and a national headquarters has been quietly opened
in Washington across from the Mayflower hotel. . . .

Here comes a group of reformers who . . . are veterans of
what we were once pleased to call the New Left, of old and
honorable battles for civil rights and against poverty and the
war in Vietnam. Today they represent the New Improved
Left: A cadre of environmentalists and decentralists, with a
political agenda for the Eighties that bears little resemblance
to that of the Sixties.

A working paper drafted by the Citizens Committee tells
the story. Among other things, it calls for:

☐ "Public control of the energy industries.

☐ "A swift halt to nuclear power.

☐ "A strong push for conservation and solar energy.

☐ "An immediate, sharp reversal in the rate of military
spending.

☐ "Stable prices for the basic necessities of life: food,
fuel, housing, medical care."

Underlying these points is the committee's perception of
democracy as a victim of both big government and especially
big business. "Elevating the national interest above vested
private interests is the heart of what the Citizens Party is
about," says the working paper. "We believe in citizen con-

[4] Excerpted from magazine article "Dreams of a Third Party," by Richard J.
Margolis, staff columnist. New Leader. 62:10–11. S. 10, '79. Reprinted with permission
from The New Leader. Copyright © 1979 by the American Labor Conference on International Affairs, Inc. All rights reserved.

trol of major investment and resource decisions. We want to see that control as decentralized as possible. Experiments in worker and community ownership should be encouraged . . . ."

Such populist notions, of course, are hardly new, but the tone of voice throughout this working paper is surprisingly measured and moderate. It reflects the new political group's leadership, which by and large consists of intellectual activists who have spent years pondering America's sundry dilemmas. The 25-person steering committee, for example, includes: Richard Barnet, author of *Global Reach* and a founder of the Institute for Policy Studies; Robert Browne, president of the Black Economic Research Center; Robert Chlopak, director of the National Public Interest Research Group (a Nader spinoff); Robert Fahs, an officer in the United Auto Workers; Jeff Faux, an economist with the Exploratory Project on Economic Alternatives; Adam Hochschild, publisher of *Mother Jones* magazine; David Hunter, director of the Stern Fund; Maggie Kuhn, head of the Gray Panthers; Edward Sadlowski, of the United Steel Workers; and Studs Terkel, the writer.

. . . The Citizens Party . . . office, tucked away on the third floor of a building that also houses the opulent Chez Camille restaurant, is the very model of a minor party's new headquarters—small, crowded and lined with hopeful legends. A large bulletin board displays news clips from around the country, including a characteristically alliterative item from *Time* magazine that calls the new venture "a Quixotic quest." A Los Angeles *Times* headline warns: "Look Out Democrats! The Citizens Party Is on Its Way." The Chicago *Tribune* complains: "A Third Party May Not Be a Joke."

Strictly speaking, as my friend Harriet Barlow patiently explained to me, the organizing committee does not consider itself a third party, there being these days only one other party to choose from, the one that some call Republican and others call Democratic. Because the two parties take nearly identical positions on most major issues, said Harriet, who is a co-chairperson of the Citizens Committee, millions of discouraged Americans have broken their voting habit. Only about one-third of all eligible voters, she reminded me, bothered to cast ballots in the last Presidential election.

So, like all newcomers on the American political stage, the Citizens Party claims to offer us a choice, not an echo. And nowadays, Harriet noted, the real choices are seldom mentioned: "Congress debates the oil question as if the only alternatives are between laissez faire and a windfall profits tax. Nobody brings up the possibility of divestiture, of workers owning the oil companies, of citizen control. The windfall tax is seen by the public as a far-Left position when it should be considered somewhere in the middle."

"Similarly," Harriet continued, "the debate over Chrysler is limited to the question of subsidy vs. no subsidy. Our leaders don't see the opportunities that Chrysler's problems present us with—opportunities for new experiments in worker control and ownership." All of this, she concluded, comes under the heading of the public's "acquiescence to the corporate definition of its need," which in turn leads to "the fraudulence of the parameters of dialogue."

After Harriet left, I talked for awhile to the Citizens Committee executive secretary, Dan Leahy, an appealing gentleman from Wenatchee, Washington. He had brown, fuzzy hair, a bushy moustache, and was wearing bluejeans with a matching jacket and cap. The party's toughest task, he told me, would be getting on the ballot in all 50 states: "Every state has different rules, and nearly all are rigged to favor the major parties. It's a nightmare."

I asked Leahy if he really expected the Citizens Party to elect a President in 1980. "We're in this for the long haul," he said. "We'll make gains in 1980, and maybe in 1984 we can win." Leahy showed me a statement by Barry Commoner that compared the Citizens Party of 1979 with the Republican Party of 1854: "We view this in many ways as parallel to the moment 125 years ago when a small group of people met in a Wisconsin town to form a new political party. They founded the Republican Party because neither of the country's major parties were confronting the great national issue of the day: slavery."

... Analogies can be helpful, but it takes a considerable glossing of history to equate the Citizens Party's chances today with the Republican triumph 125 years ago. For one thing, the party the Republicans were hoping to replace—the Whigs—was already conveniently bankrupt; by 1854, when that historic meeting in Ripon, Wisconsin, took place, the Whigs' dissolution seemed assured, and even a conservative like Edward Bates was ready to bolt to a new party.

For another thing, the slavery issue back then was far more critical and divisive than are any current issues, including energy and inflation. Slavery had been debated and disputed for more than half a century; the Whigs had spent two decades staking their political reputations on their ability to settle the argument through negotiation and compromise. By 1854 it was clear to nearly everyone that they had failed, and that a fresh political alliance was required—not a small band of reformers, but a broad coalition of free-soilers and Northern industrialists, the latter being less interested in abolitionism than in protective tariffs and expansion of the railroads.

Then, too, there remains the question of whether *any* group today—even one more broad-based and more richly endowed than the Citizens Party—can succeed in ousting either of the major parties. Those Ripon Republicans, after all, were the last to turn the trick, though many since have made the attempt. Not even Teddy Roosevelt could do it.

It is true, I think, what the Citizens Party says of our two Establishment parties: That they are without great and guiding principles; that their positions on most major questions are essentially identical; that they offer few authentic choices to the thoughtful voter. But what else is new?

There are now two great and several minor parties in the United States [noted the Englishman James Bryce in *The American Commonwealth* (1907)]. The great parties are the Republicans and the Democrats. What are their principles, their distinctive tenets, their tendencies? ... This is what a European is always asking of intelligent Republicans and intelligent Democrats. He is always asking because he never gets an answer ... After some months the truth begins to dawn on him . . . neither party has any principles, any distinctive tenets . . . .

The parties with principles, Bryce observed sadly and condescendingly, were invariably weak: The Socialists, the Populists, the Greenbackers, the Prohibitionists. But what Bryce failed to point out was that the programs of those splinter groups often found their way into the platforms of the two major parties. The Democrats in particular have been able over the years to borrow doctrines and ideas from the maverick Left and consequently to reinvent themselves from one generation to the next. In the 1930s, for example, the Democrats in effect created a new major party as an alternative to the third-party Socialists, who polled more than a million votes in 1932.

The test of Citizens Party success, therefore, will not be whether they win or lose but whether they can get big enough and noisy enough to scare the hell out of the Democrats. I wish them luck.

THE D.S.O.C.—RADICALS ON A TIGHTROPE[5]

There was a moment at the close of the Democratic Party's midterm convention in Memphis last December [1978] when Ben Wattenberg of the Coalition for a Democratic Majority, secure in the knowledge that nothing the convention had done would make the world any less safe for neoconservatism, paused to speak with Michael Harrington who, along with the United Auto Workers' Douglas Fraser, had been the left's primary spokesman from the convention floor.

"Mike," said Wattenberg, "you guys are on the map now."

It was, of course, just a remark made in passing; it was also

[5] Reprint of magazine article "Socialism Comes Out: The D.S.O.C.—Radicals on a Tightrope," by Harold Meyerson, Los Angeles-based free-lance journalist and member of the D.S.O.C. national board. *Nation.* 228:360-3. Ap. 7, '79. Copyright 1979 The Nation Associates.

a verdict that had not been passed on an American socialist movement in the last forty years.

The "you guys" in question—the Democratic Socialist Organizing Committee (D.S.O.C.), which Harrington chairs—came to Houston in February [1979] to chart a course for the next two years, debate issues, educate one another, renew old friendships and make new ones, and—the distinguishing feature of the convention—to deal with the unaccustomed pleasures, responsibilities and perils of being on the map.

In the six years since the D.S.O.C. was formed out of the antiwar minority of the old Socialist Party, it has grown from a faction of 200—"the defeated remnant of a defeated remnant," Harrington had called them—to an organization of 3,000 whose members include Gloria Steinem, Julian Bond, Victor Gotbaum, Robert Lekachman, Berkeley's Ronald Dellums (the first member of a socialist organization to sit in Congress since 1926), who delivered an extraordinary address to the convention, and the president of a million-member union, William Winpisinger of the International Association of Machinists and Aerospace Workers, who is now also one of the D.S.O.C.'s five vice chairmen.

But 3,000 members scarcely constitute a movement, and no number of luminaries could of themselves restore socialism to a place in the American political spectrum. If the D.S.O.C. is on the map, it is in part the result of a political strategy that has placed it both at the center and on the left of the mainstream left. It is an anomalous but by no means untenable position, and understandably it was the subject of some debate at the Houston convention.

For the D.S.O.C., the reconstruction of an American socialist movement begins with the simple recognition that there is such a thing as American exceptionalism—not, to be sure, as an eternal given of American social reality but most surely as a prevailing, if reversible, political condition. For a variety of reasons, prominent among which is the long record of failures of previous socialist movements, the forces that can provide the impetus for any social democratization in this nation are not themselves socialist. The task of the socialist thus becomes, in Harrington's phrase, to walk a tightrope—to work within the reformist left for radical restructuring, to be in the liberal community but not of it, to participate in working-class struggles for incremental change without losing sight of the socialist vision.

A major implication of this analysis has been to make the Democratic Party, alas, the arena in which the D.S.O.C. engages in electoral politics (and this "alas" is virtually an official position with the committee, a consensus "alas"); and it is within Democratic politics that it has achieved its breakthrough. Its activities began quite modestly with the election of a few members as delegates to the party's 1974 midterm convention, where they conducted an official session on economic planning. In 1976, the D.S.O.C. pulled together a coalition of union, minority group and party reform leaders that used the platform proceedings and a rally at the New York National Convention to promote the cause of planned full employment. This coalition was given a more permanent structure in 1977, when the D.S.O.C. formed the Democratic Agenda. An Agenda-sponsored full-employment conference held in Washington in the autumn of that year brought together the broadest coalition of progressive forces the nation had seen since the 1960s (and in so doing laid the groundwork for Douglas Fraser's Progressive Alliance).

By the 1978 Memphis midterm convention, the Democratic Agenda had expanded its focus from employment to a whole range of progressive causes; it served at the convention as the surrogate for all left opposition to the Carter Administration. Two of the three opposition resolutions that were brought to the floor by petition were Democratic Agenda resolutions (they called for a public energy corporation and for an inflation policy that constrained corporate control of prices), as were all six of the other opposition resolutions that the Administration either compromised on or accepted in order to avoid a fight. Five hundred of the 1,500 delegates present in Memphis (thirty of them from the D.S.O.C.) attended the Agenda's caucus and voted with the Agenda on the convention floor.

So Harrington was by no means exaggerating when he asserted in his keynote address at Houston that this one D.S.O.C. program has become "the programmatic center of the Democratic left within the Democratic Party." It is a highly unusual role for a socialist organization to play; yet one of the stories of Houston was the breadth of support that was accorded this strategy even as its nuances were debated. The convention manifesto of the D.S.O.C.'s self-styled "left-socialist group," for instance, called upon the committee to articulate more explicitly socialist positions within its coalition work, but also specifically endorsed the continuation of that work. Indeed, the convention ratified without opposition a proposal that could heighten the D.S.O.C.'s status as the left's programmatic center: the transformation of the Democratic Agenda into a multi-city political barnstorming "Program in Search of a President and Congress" campaign that will mobilize the left for the 1980 wars.

For if the Democratic Agenda has not induced an identity crisis within a renewed American socialism—and it has not—it is largely because the mainstream left in which the socialists operate has itself been forced in the last few years to move beyond the confines of traditional welfare-state liberalism. The A.F.L.-C.I.O. position on controls, after all, calls for subjecting the entire economy to a politically determined incomes policy. The issues around which the Democratic Agenda rallied the liberal community at Memphis and elsewhere—planned full employment, public energy, an end to corporate control of markets—may not, as Harrington noted, be very radical for a socialist movement but they do indicate a movement on the part of the left to supplant some portion of corporate power with some level of social control.

The leftward movement of the mainline left has been crucial to the D.S.O.C.'s evolution, enabling it to function within a predominantly liberal community even while intensifying its critique of liberalism. "The liberal vacuum in society historically tends to be filled by radicals," observed historian Jim

Chapin, who as a leading D.S.O.C. activist and as chairman of the New York State New Democratic Coalition (the reform Democrats) is no stranger to the varieties of socialist-liberal interaction. "Some become liberals, some wear liberal masks." Yet there was little of either in Houston. "American liberalism still basically adheres to the New Deal strategy of leaving the corporate infrastructure alone," Harrington noted, and it is precisely this strategy, he contended, that has caused the stagflation that has placed liberalism into eclipse.

For it is stagflation, the stranglehold wedlock of recession and inflation, that has pushed the left in the direction of structural change, brought about the conservative resurgence and so rearranged the political landscape that, as Ronald Dellums put it in Houston, "the middle of American politics has vanished." For forty years, that middle had given its support to a limited, begrudging welfare state that propped up purchasing power just enough to head off depressions, as well as to a corporate sector that was developing an increasing immunity to the vagaries of the marketplace.

In the last half-decade, the inflationary pressures built into this tradeoff have become severe. Citing the corporations' ability to raise prices during the 1974 recession and their creation of an international dollar market that is beyond the manipulative capacities of the Federal Reserve, Harrington labeled the liberal position on corporations little short of suicidal: "The structural transformations of the economy," he contended, "have subverted both the theory and the practice of the New Deal." In effect, the social contract to which the middle of the spectrum has given its allegiance since the 1930s is up for renegotiation. For the first time in forty years, then, the welfare state is under serious attack. For the first time in forty years, American labor leaders talk of class warfare. For the first time in forty years, a socialist organization can play a significant role on the American left—a development that Chapin placed in dialectical perspective. "We're the antithesis," he said, "to the New Right."

So a capitalist crisis has created the preconditions for socialism's return to the map—the same capitalist crisis that has placed Wattenberg's neoconservative brethren currently in the ascendancy (a causal analysis they doubtless would dispute). If the economic ideas in widest circulation no longer come from centrist economists of the [Paul A.] Samuelson school but rather from the monetarist school of Milton Friedman and Arthur Laffer, it is also the case that the economic ideas in widest circulation on the mainstream left come from socialists such as Robert Heilbroner, Robert Lekachman, Leslie Nulty (whose "sectoral" analysis of inflation is ubiquitous throughout the left today) and Lester Thurow. Business leaders increasingly seek the services of sophisticated union busters; labor leaders are beginning to turn again to the radicals. Indeed, a convention high point was the declaration of Bill Holayter, political action director of the Machinists (a declaration that came complete with his phone number), that he would put Machinist locals in touch with D.S.O.C. locals throughout the country.

One sign of the socialists' growing acceptance throughout much of the left is the modest but increasing success of their own campaigns for office. Since the D.S.O.C.'s 1977 Chicago convention, members have been elected to school boards, city councils, state legislatures. Zoltan Ferency of the D.S.O.C. placed second among four candidates in Michigan's Democratic gubernatorial primary last year with 25 percent of the vote. Whether there would be equivalent mass left support for a Harrington or a Dellums campaign in next year's Democratic Presidential primaries is another question. Urged last November by the D.S.O.C. National Board to consider a candidacy in the absence of a serious progressive alternative, Harrington took soundings that led him to conclude his base of support was as yet too narrow. It is, however, a fluid situation, and neither Harrington nor Dellums has ruled out running should more support be forthcoming.

But perhaps the most striking development since the Chicago convention has occurred within the organization itself. Like so many of its predecessors on the American left, the D.S.O.C. was an organization whose national strategy preceded any significant accumulation of members. Even after it began to grow, its national political activities were its primary focus, and members were seldom afforded any opportunity to involve themselves in activities specifically related to the organization: "What do D.S.O.C. members do?" was a question often posed to members, frequently by their fellow members. In the last two years, however, the scope of the committee's activities has greatly expanded, often in some surprising directions. Even members familiar with many aspects of the new growth were struck in Houston by, as one member put it, "the evidence of activity all over the map." It is a remark that can be misconstrued to refer to the D.S.O.C.'s genuinely national presence: there are now more than forty locals in more than thirty states, engaged in pursuits ranging from organizing the unemployed, which they have attempted with some modest success in Philadelphia, to assembling a solar energy coalition that includes both the Building Trades Council and the Clamshell Alliance, a small-scale miracle wrought in Boston.

More significantly, the "activity all over the map" may signal the beginning of the end of socialism's long isolation from a number of potentially radical constituencies. The D.S.O.C. has a growing Hispanic caucus, which conducted a convention rally in the Houston *barrio*, and which publishes a journal reflecting the diversity of a membership that comes from the Cuban exile community of Miami and the desolation of the South Bronx. There is a Religion and Socialism Committee with wide representation from the Catholic and Protestant left and among liberation theologists; its Houston caucus was addressed by D.S.O.C. member Harvey Cox, professor of theology at the Harvard Divinity School. There is for the first time an active and sizable youth section stirring on supposedly somnolent campuses.

There are continuing failures of outreach, too, the most obvious being the inability to recruit any significant number of blacks. There has been an increase, however, in recruitment from another constituency from which many Democratic socialists and trade unionists were estranged during the 1960s: the survivors of the New Left, for whom totalitarian left regimes of the second and third world no longer serve as models. "Precisely because we have moved into the position of dealing with the center of American politics," says outgoing National Secretary Jack Clark, "we have attracted people to our left."

But it is more than that, for it is also true that the D.S.O.C.'s founders, some of whom waged sectarian wars of varying degrees of justification from the 1930s through the 1960s, have been explicitly committed since the committee's founding to preserving a pluralistic organization. Indeed, the convention overwhelmingly ratified a proposal to investigate the possibility of a merger with the 800-member New American Movement, an organization that emerged from the remnants of the New Left in the early 1970s. (The merger may founder, however, on the unwillingness of some within the N.A.M. to work inside either the Democratic Party or the Socialist International, to which the D.S.O.C. gained admittance last year.)

It is the absence of self-righteous sectarian rhetoric from the D.S.O.C.'s internal debates that is so striking to a member of the Veterans of Sectarian Wars at his first look. For the sizable number of 20-year-olds who came to Houston, the D.S.O.C. may be the first national left organization to have flourished during their political lifetimes, but for the survivors of so many burnt-out movements who were present in Houston in far greater numbers, the D.S.O.C. has become a kind of unexpected last chance they are determined not to throw away, least of all in a moment of unyielding purity. In the words of Detroit auto worker Roger Robinson, one of its founding members, the D.S.O.C. is "an organization of people schooled in defeat." Their knowledge of history complements their sense of decency, and this is one final reason why socialism has regained a place, however precarious, on the American map.

THE NEW RIGHT TAKES AIM[6]

Block the SALT treaty? "We'll fight it to the end," says Howard Phillips, 38, a husky Bostonian who heads one of the ultraconservative groups that are raising millions to oppose ratification. "In the long run we lose only if we fail to fight."

Unite Protestant fundamentalists and Catholic ethnics into a political bloc by emphasizing emotional "family" issues? "A year or two ago nothing was happening," says Paul Weyrich, 36, a former TV reporter who leads another right-wing organization. "Now we're moving."

Chop down some of the Senate's most prominent Democrats? "Of course, we can do it," says Terry Dolan, 28, chairman of a third ultraconservative organization. "We are out to destroy the popularity ratings of several liberal Senators, and it's working. Frank Church is screaming like a stuck pig, and I don't blame him."

Brash young leaders with small offices and big dreams—these are the centurions of the movement that claims the title of America's New Right. Its general goals, a drastic reduction in domestic government activity and a hard anti-Communist line abroad, are familiar enough. So is its rhetoric. But the New Right has developed some fresh, effective tactics. It scored a few surprising electoral upsets last year, and now it smells blood.

Kentucky Senator Wendell Ford, head of the Senate Democratic Campaign Committee, warns that his party's control of the upper house is under serious threat for the first time in a quarter-century. Party Tactician Terry O'Connell, observing that House Democrats are also worried, says: "Everyone I know is scared to death of this thing." Senior Correspondent Laurence I. Barrett explored the reasons for this anxiety. His report:

[6] Reprint of staff-written magazine article. *Time.* 114:20-1. Ag. 20, '79. Reprinted by permission from TIME, The Weekly Newsmagazine; Copyright Time Inc. 1979.

Conservatives who succeeded in nominating Senator Barry Goldwater for President 15 years ago sought power through control of the Republican Party. In the mid-'70s, there was a feeble effort to unite diverse factions into a national conservative party. Today's New Right has different priorities. It stresses 1) the creation of coalitions among special interest groups, 2) support or opposition on specific legislation and 3) concentration on Senate and House seats that can be won. Says William Rusher, publisher of *National Review* and an admiring expert on the movement: "These are the first conservative groups that really have got down to electoral and legislative nitty-gritty."

Though the organizational network is loose and right-wing groups must compete with each other for contributions, the leaders often confer on policy and tactics. Frequently the host is Richard Viguerie, 45, the direct-mail conglomerateur whose enterprises in Falls Church, Va., are expected to gross nearly $20 million this year. Viguerie, who said last week that he will work for the John Connally campaign, is at once an adviser, technician and promoter for the New Right. In his mass mailings and monthly *Conservative Digest*—an indulgence that ran up a $1.5 million loss last year—Viguerie plugs the newest and most active groups. Several of them are his paying clients. The three most important organizations have all been formed since 1974. They are:

☐ The Conservative Caucus, ostensibly nonpartisan, concentrates on national issues and local organization rather than elections. It claims 300,000 dues-paying members ($5 to $15), maintains coordinators in 40 states and committees in 250 congressional districts. The caucus produces a raft of literature on the voting records of individual legislators and "fact sheets" on controversial questions. The summaries give both sides of the issue, but leave no doubt where virtue lies. An item on federal assistance to New York City is accompanied by a cartoon portraying the city as a prostitute. A piece on abortion in military hospitals shows a baby being put into a trash can with a bayonet. The caucus helped lead the fight against the Panama Canal treaties, and is now organizing opposition to SALT II with a Viguerie direct-mail campaign and a series of seminars around the country.

The caucus' mainspring is Phillips, once a conventional Republican who chaired the party in Boston and then served in the Nixon Administration as head of the Office of Economic Opportunity. That experience soured him on traditional bureaucracy.

Disillusioned with both Nixon and Ford, Phillips is now an enrolled Democrat. Says he: "To the extent that there is an opposition to the failed liberalism of our generation, that opposition comes from the New Right rather than the Republican Party." Losing on any single issue matters little, Phillips preaches, since each conflict generates opposition to the status quo and support for the New Right. He cites the example of an airline pilot who worked for the caucus two years ago on the Panama question and was drawn into politics. The pilot, Republican Gordon Humphrey, is now the junior U.S. Senator from New Hampshire.

□ Committee for the Survival of a Free Congress emphasizes campaign organization and funding. Last year it donated $400,000 in cash and services to right-wing congressional candidates and it maintains ten field coordinators who work in primaries and general elections.

Survival's chief is Weyrich, a former Republican Senate staff aide who is considered the best strategist of the new generation. A Greek Catholic, Weyrich began the effort to involve prominent Evangelical Fundamentalists in right-wing politics. He also took the lead in defining "family issues"—including abortion and gay rights—as a rallying point for voters who are not necessarily conservative on other questions. With the cooperation of Phillips' Caucus, that effort led to the creation last month of still another group, Moral Majority. One of its founders is Jerry Falwell of Lynchburg, Va., whose *Old-Time Gospel Hour* makes him one of the most prominent electronic preachers in the U.S. Falwell envisions a mass organization including Baptists, Catholics, Mormons and Orthodox Jews. His goal: "To defend the free enterprise system, the family, Bible morality, fundamental values."

☐ National Conservative Political Action Committee (N.C.P.A.C.) also collects funds nationwide to target in specific campaigns, but it emphasizes publicity rather than precinct organization. Thanks to the brass of its chairman, Dolan, N.C.P.A.C. lately has drawn more fire from its foes than other conservative groups. The notoriety, including an attack against it in last month's AFL-CIO political newsletter, helps in the competition for conservative dollars. N.C.P.A.C. can use the money. Debts forced Dolan to suspend his own $2,000-a-month salary this summer, and he is trying to raise $700,000 for the opening shots of his "Target '80" effort to defeat five prominent Democratic Senators: Frank Church of Idaho, Alan Cranston of California, George McGovern of South Dakota, John Culver of Iowa and Birch Bayh of Indiana.

Dolan got into politics as a Republican volunteer in his native state of Connecticut and at 21 was a paid organizer in the 1972 Nixon campaign. "I'm ashamed to admit that now," he says. In 1976, as a protest gesture against the major parties, he voted for the Libertarians. Says he: "The Republican Party is a fraud. It's a social club where rich people go to pick their noses."

Despite such contempt for the G.O.P.—a feeling returned by many in the Republican Establishment—the party is the short-term beneficiary of much of the movement's activities. True, Viguerie is taking on more Democratic House candidates as clients. But most of the New Right hit lists feature only Democrats.

The most important is Church. According to the congressional scorecards maintained by both liberal and conservative lobbying organizations, Church is closer to the Democratic center than to the left. But because of his celebrity as chairman of the Foreign Relations Committee, defeating him would be a big victory for the New Right. And he is particularly vulnerable because Idaho usually votes conservative in federal elections.

Dolan's approach is to start early and hit hard on the incumbent's record. An N.C.P.A.C. affiliate in Idaho began TV and radio commercials in June. Initially Church was accused of having "almost always opposed a strong national defense." The TV spot was taped in front of an empty ICBM silo, implying that Church's attitude was responsible for the void. In fact, the silo was part of the obsolescent Titan system, which has been mostly replaced by Minuteman missiles. A mailing prepared for N.C.P.A.C. by Viguerie calls Church "the radical . . . who singlehanded has presided over the destruction of the FBI and the CIA." Church protests that his enemies are using "the big-lie technique."

Dolan can spend as much as he raises, despite the federal restriction that normally limits one political action committee to $10,000 per candidate. The reason is that N.C.P.A.C. is exploiting the "independent expenditure" loophole permitted under a 1976 Supreme Court ruling. This allows free spending provided that there is no connection between the advertiser and the political beneficiary of the advertising. In Idaho, Church does not even have an announced opponent yet. His probable rival is Republican Congressman Steven Symms, who says that he has "no reason to be interested in a dirty campaign" against Church.

That's fine with Dolan, who tells a group of prospective N.C.P.A.C. contributors: "Steve Symms will never have to say anything negative about Frank Church. We'll talk about all the negative stuff." And in Idaho, where air time is cheap, N.C.P.A.C. will talk about its view of Church's record over and over. One radio spot was aired 150 times a day throughout the state for five days. The cost was just $4,000. Predicts Dolan: "By 1980 there will be people voting against Church without remembering why."

While N.C.P.A.C. wages war with words, others affiliated with the New Right are attempting to organize single-interest groups against Church. A new antiabortion group called Stop the Baby Killers, with Idaho Congressman George Hansen as honorary chairman, describes Church, Culver and Bayh as "men who apparently think it's perfectly okay to slaughter unborn infants." In fact, Church favors a constitutional amendment that would outlaw abortion in most circumstances. He is also opposed to controls on firearms. But the Citizens Committee for the Right to Keep and Bear Arms, a national group with an active chapter in Idaho, finds him wanting. Says its chairman, Alan Gottlieb: "There's no question that Steve Symms would be a better Senator on our issue. Church votes the way he does because he'd be tarred and feathered if he didn't." The National Right to Work Committee, Stop ERA and other single-issue groups are expected to work against Church and most of the other "targeted" Democrats as well.

The ferocity of this assault may turn out to be an error. The intended victims have begun organizing their re-election campaigns earlier than they would in a "normal" pre-election year. N.C.P.A.C.'s gambit is also causing dissension among New Right strategists, who are not as united as they seem. Weyrich's newsletter openly criticized Dolan's approach in Idaho and warned that he risked a backlash favoring Church. Weyrich's apprehension that Church may be perceived as the home-town underdog being attacked by alien bullies matches exactly Church's own strategy for survival.

NEOCONSERVATISM: WHICH PARTY'S LINE?[7]

Even before Irving Kristol and his fellow neoconservatives were apotheosized on the cover of *Esquire* magazine recently, students of contemporary political polemics were aware that this new breed of conservative was well on the way toward winning a war of literary and philosophical attrition. The exhaustion of orthodox liberal thought has become a commonplace. When, for example, has anyone read an intellectually respectable, emotionally compelling defense of the liberal

[7] Reprint of magazine article by Karl O'Lessker, senior editor, *American Spectator,* and professor of public and environmental affairs, Indiana University. *American Spectator.* 12:8–10. Mr. '79. Copyright The American Spectator 1979. Reprinted by permission.

welfare state, comparable in quality, say, to Arthur Schlesinger, Jr.'s *The Vital Center*, now more than a quarter of a century old? (The Marxists still maintain some semblance of vitality—Michael Harrington, for one—and a crypto-socialist like Galbraith has finally stopped being crypto, though he has taken to affirming his collectivist vision at a time of declining power and impaired eyesight.) While one may get the impression from reading the *New York Times* that there is a viable liberal-intellectual alternative, it almost always turns out to be socialist—but the *New York Times* doesn't seem to know the difference. For anyone not yet convinced of the intellectual dominance of neoconservativism today, it will be a helpful exercise to draw up a list of persons in the liberal, non-Marxist camp who compare in academic weight and intellectual stature to Edward Banfield, Daniel Bell, Nathan Glazer, Irving Kristol, Lewis Lapham, Seymour Martin Lipset, Robert Nisbet, Norman Podhoretz, Nelson Polsby, Aaron Wildavsky, and James Q. Wilson.

That is an impressive but also a very diverse list of intellectual heavyweights. What unites them, what has earned them the common label "neoconservative," is a set of highly prudential approaches to policy that include most particularly a deep skepticism about the ability of big government to accomplish very much of what it sets out to accomplish, a profound suspicion as to the humanitarian and pacific impulses of Soviet Communism, and a healthy respect, almost Burkean in intensity, for tradition and social order.

It is the first of these characteristics that is most immediately relevant to the domestic policy battles that appear to be shaping up for the next few years. Its flavor has been neatly captured by Everett Carll Ladd in the form of a series of rhetorical questions he attributes to leading neoconservative publicists:

Hasn't the New Deal state, they ask, been "Balkanized" programmatically, broken into a series of small units each manipulated by a cluster of special interests? . . . Aren't public bureaucracies, by their very size and insulation, inherently unresponsive to popular wishes? Haven't so many government intrusions been fostered as to incapacitate the private economic system in a number of critical areas? Doesn't the secular march of government spending, absolutely and as a relative slice of the gross national product, expose the United States to the economic disorder known as the "English sickness"?

No doubt a large minority of the American public, Democrats as well as independents and Republicans, would answer those questions in the affirmative, but that is not the present point, at least not directly. Our concern here is with political process: How, exactly, can neoconservative doctrine have an impact on public policy?

One kind of answer comes out of a marriage of Charles Dickens and John Maynard Keynes. It was Dickens' Mr. Micawber who kept expressing his confidence that "something will turn up." And it was Keynes who talked of the hard-headed politicians of one generation being unwitting slaves to the ideas of "academic scribblers" of another. So if the academic scribblers of neoconservativism continue to hammer away with anything like their current level of eloquence and rate of production, something may indeed—almost certainly will—turn up in the way of public policy.

A different, more direct kind of answer involves the political parties and the possibility of neoconservative influence on one or both of them. For even if we accord a fair degree of long-term plausibility to the Dickens-Keynes scenario, we still have to recognize that liberals continue to dominate the policy-making machinery of the federal government; and neither Proposition 13 fever nor President Carter's newfound commitment to budget "austerity" holds forth much promise of prying liberal hands away from the levers of power. Amidst all the hullabaloo about the welcome defeat last year of a few Senate liberals, not many people paid much attention to the far more significant changes that have taken place within both houses, whereby liberal Democrats have replaced conservative Democrats in key committee and subcommittee chairmanships; Edward Kennedy's replacement of James Eastland as chairman of the Senate Judiciary Committee is only the most visible of the dozens that have occurred practically unnoticed outside Washington. Policy-making remains firmly in the grip of congressional and bureaucratic liberals. That will change only through either mass conversion of the electorally dominant Democrats, or revitalization of the Republican Party such that it might once again control both Congress and the White House at the same time—a dispensation it has not enjoyed since 1954, and before that since 1930.

Given the apparently insurmountable electoral odds, it is tempting to conclude that the great policy battles of the neoconservatives and liberals over the next decade or so will be fought out, not *between* parties, but *within* the majority Democratic Party. Not only is there precedent for this; one of our most insightful political analysts, Samuel Lubell, said in his great 1951 book, *The Future of American Politics*, that this is in fact the norm:

Our political solar system . . . has been characterized not by two equally competing suns, but by a sun and a moon. It is within the majority party that the issues of any particular period are fought out; while the minority party shines in the reflected radiance of the heat thus generated.

Moreover, the Republican Party has for many years been something less than hospitable to the clash of ideas. Its leadership generally has had about as much use and respect for intellectuals as for welfare mothers. Everett Ladd, in his *Fortune* article of late 1977, was surely not far from the mark when he noted that "The G.O.P. has been routed so thoroughly within the intellectual community that it finds itself confined to a spectator role in the great unfolding debate [between neoconservatives and the traditional Left]." (There is some encouraging evidence to the contrary, however. Of great importance is the rise in policy influence of the American Enterprise Institute, with its stable of intellectuals and academicians, most of whom have Republican Party leanings. And the Republican National Committee itself has recently begun publication of a journal called *Commonsense*, which looks to be an intellectually respectable forum for the dissemination of, believe it or not, *ideas.*)

A related point has to do with the dynamics of what Nelson Polsby has called the "one-and-one-half party system," a phenomenon with which Americans have long been familiar at the level of state politics. Put simply, in a party system in which one party is consistently, almost unchallengeably stronger than the other, new brains and talent will tend to flow into the stronger party and thus add to its advantage. That is not an iron law, of course; it is an accurate statement of tendency. And it highlights a profoundly important truth about political party federalism: Federalism itself is the surest guarantor of a viable two-party system; for even in times of one-party domination at the national level, the minority party may remain powerful within a number of states and serve as a magnet and training-ground for fresh talent. Conversely, with the disintegration of previously secure areas for the nationally minority party, that vital form of insurance tends to ebb away. It is for this reason that the Republican Party may be in danger of practically ceasing to exist (although it may well be true, as Ronald Reagan's campaign manager, John Sears, has said, that "The Republican Party is like a fungus. It may look dead but you can never kill it").

And yet for anyone who has paid even passing attention to Democratic Party affairs at the national level, it is difficult to envision the beast as a suitable mount for neoconservative riders. With utter insouciance Democratic members of Congress each year vote additional billions of dollars at the behest of the great Treasury-raiding interest groups; and they do so without ever inquiring as to how the bureaucracy intends to go about translating the Congress's good intentions and the taxpayers' money into—what? Jobs for the unemployed? Rebuilt cities? Economic development in depressed areas? The billions flow out and the votes flow in, and little if anything happens for the benefit of the nominal beneficiaries.

Consider as well the example of Senator Daniel Patrick Moynihan, who has provided neoconservatism with so much of its characteristic tone and eloquence. Today, for the first time in his distinguished career, he is an elected official, whose New York constituents are among the most liberal in the nation. How does Moynihan's voting record in the Senate differ from that of any other liberal Eastern Democrat? Except on national security matters, it doesn't. Few, if any, of his votes on domestic policy betray an interest in impeding the growth of the federal government or making it easier for the private sector to grow and flourish. And the reason, certainly, is not because he is a hypocrite or a weakling or a turncoat, but because of the imperatives of Democratic electability in states like New York and an increasing number of others. In short, the ideas of neoconservative policy intellectuals may well be "unavailable" to elected Democrats. How then are those ideas to get into the policy stream?

The answer, I believe, lies with the saving remnant of the Republican Party, with moderates like Robert Packwood in the Senate and Willis Gradison in the House, and conservatives like Richard Lugar in the Senate and Jack Kemp in the House. These are men of intellectual weight and some influence. They are of proven electability in their own constituencies. Their voices are heard in party councils. I have no idea whether they will even try to build, let alone succeed in building, a programmatic base—fashioned out of essentially neoconservative ideas—on which most elected Republicans can stand. But there are a couple of highly practical political reasons for thinking that a Republican resurgence based on neoconservative policies may be a live possibility in the near term. One is precisely the desperately low state of the Republican Party fortunes, as evidenced not only by its disproportionally low numbers of officeholders across the country, but also by its failure to do any better than it did at the polls last November. Absent a more impressive turnabout than that, its fortunes are bound to sink even lower. And what can possibly stimulate that more impressive turnabout other than vital new ideas attractively presented? By contrast, the Democrats are caught in the toils of their own success, and are hardly likely as a party to follow the example of Jerry Brown in casting aside what has after all been a winning formula— "Borrow and borrow, spend and spend, elect and elect."

Secondly, by neat dialectical antithesis to what I have just said, the enormous budget deficits of recent years have finally

begun to take their toll on public well-being. Liberal economists may be captivated by such theological constructs as the
so-called "full-employment budget," but an increasing number of plain citizens are coming round to the view that large
deficits contribute largely to inflation. And it is inflation that
holds first rank in every opinion poll of citizen concerns. In
short, the Democrats are vulnerable at the very heart of their
public philosophy and programs. They can be attacked with
great effect on the consequence of their most characteristic
policies—so long as the attack is not directed at the funda-
mentals of our American version of the welfare state. As Governor Reagan doubtless learned in New Hampshire three
years ago, proposals to turn over to the states $90 billion
worth of social spending, including social security, medicare,
and unemployment compensation, amount to an exquisitely
calculated formula for snatching electoral defeat from the
jaws of victory.

An assault on the federally administered welfare state is
no part of neoconservative doctrine. No one could allege that
a Kristol or a Glazer or a Banfield wants to repeal the New
Deal. The sort of policies that neoconservative Republicans
might advocate would involve incremental changes in the
rate of growth of federal expenditures on social programs,
coupled with careful dismantling of much of the stifling federal regulatory apparatus. Probably, too, there would be proposals to modify minimum-wage laws so as to restore some
labor-market value to unskilled teenagers, to tinker with the
welfare system so as to make it worth people's while to seek
employment, and in general to invest the private sector with
greater responsibilities and opportunities for seeing to the
nation's economic health. None of this may sound very controversial to most audiences, but it is safe to predict that the
roars of protest from politically well-muscled groups would
be thunderous, perhaps even—literally—riotous. And therefore we should expect none but a brave, skillful, and determined political leadership to bring it off.

Today the working and middle classes are growing restive
under a burden of inflation and taxation they are unable to

see as justified, and the Democrats are incapable of providing them relief—not because the party is wicked, but because it is caught up in a strangulating network of interest-group relationships and doesn't know how to break out. But at the same time the great majority of American voters will tolerate no radical assault on the welfare state. So the problem, as well as the opportunity, for Republican ascent to the status of viable opposition comes down to that party's ability to formulate coherent policies that are at once clear alternatives to liberal Democratic orthodoxy and supportive of existing institutions.

The future of American politics thus seems to lie with a renascence of the badly debilitated junior partner in our two-party system. It is surely not unreasonable to expect the rising generation of Republican leaders to identify themselves and their party with neoconservative policies, because that is the way to survive—to survive and flourish. Some may even be attracted to the notion that it is also the nation's best hope to survive and flourish as a free society. If that should happen, we may yet witness the happiest conjunction of a narrow political and broad national interest since the founding of the Republican Party itself.

III. SPECIAL-INTEREST GROUPS

EDITOR'S INTRODUCTION

The complexity of modern American society has spawned an overwhelming volume of societal issues and problems during the past decade. These issues, in turn, have led to the formation of special-interest groups, each absorbed in its own small area of concern and indifferent to other questions. Most of these groups emerge in opposition to a trend that offends their moral sensibilities. For example, antiabortionists band together to oppose what they consider to be murder, and local environmental groups organize to work against increases in industrial pollution.

The rise of special-interest groups and its disconcerting effects on beleaguered legislators is documented in the first article in this section, an analysis by the late *New Yorker* staff writer Richard Rovere; conceding that "there is no reason that those who make the laws of a nation should not be required to master its problems one at a time," he warned that the inability of zealous special-interest groups to compromise can lead to a dangerous anarchy.

Legalized abortion and sweeping tax reform—special issues that have transformed party loyalists into battalions of single-minded militants—are the subjects of two *Saturday Review* excerpts. Roger W. Williams, focusing on the politics of abortion, and David Osborne, investigating populist tax-reform movements, illustrate how an overriding issue serves to unite adherents (or opponents) in new political configurations.

Next, John Herbers, reporting for the New York *Times*, focuses on neighborhood activist groups, a "major realignment of urban political forces." He quotes urban activists who maintain that "political parties [in urban areas] are virtually powerless."

The overt and intensifying political activity of homosexuals is the subject of an article by Paul Robinson, a contributing editor of the *New Republic,* who comments on the May 1979 riot in San Francisco that followed a verdict of voluntary manslaughter, rather than murder, for the killer of the mayor and a homosexual city official. Robinson finds the riot to be a "significant moment in the evolution of political awareness among homosexuals," giving notice of the political coming of age of that sector of the city's population.

An excerpt from a *Newsweek* cover story outlines the special concerns of Western states that have molded the region into a bloc of voters opposed to many Federal policies—and to the rest of the nation. Neglect of regional problems involving land, water, and mineral resource management, the article predicts, will lead to serious political conflicts in the 1980s as Westerners press their needs.

SINGLE-ISSUE POLITICS[1]
by Richard Rovere

Meg Greenfield, who this year won a Pulitzer Prize for her editorials in the Washington *Post,* recently wrote that she could not recall a time when "interest-group issues and politics . . . dominated events" as they do today. What she meant by "interest group" was something rather different from what President Carter has in mind when he uses the term, as in his populist moods he often does. Discussing tax reform at his news conference last week, he spoke with some bitterness of lobbyists on Capitol Hill who work to preserve "special privileges for people who have them because they are so powerful and so influential now and [have been] in the past." Miss Greenfield's special interests include not only the rich and powerful but many who are anything but rich and whose

[1] Reprint of "Affairs of State" column, by the late Richard Rovere, *New Yorker* staff writer and author of books on American politics. *New Yorker.* 65:139+. My. 8, '78. Reprinted by permission; © 1978 The New Yorker Magazine, Inc.

power, such as it is, lies in numbers and determination rather than in property and entrenched privilege—civil servants, family farmers, coal miners, steelworkers, wage earners strapped by rising Social Security taxes. Their motives, of course, differ little from those of Carter's malefactors of great wealth: they want to keep what they've got and, if possible, get more. But among the interest groups so conspicuously active today are many whose members do not stand to gain or lose by the causes they espouse or oppose. The issues that have recently generated the most political heat and given rise to the most rancorous debate have little to do with anyone's profit or loss or lust for power. Neither the proponents nor the opponents of the Panama Canal treaties, for example, had any financial stake in having them voted up or down in the Senate; partisans on both sides saw the matter as one of high principle, involving differing concepts of honor, justice, pride, responsibility, and patriotism. Arms reduction on a large scale, if it ever comes, would bring distress to defense contractors, but few of those who will undoubtedly oppose a treaty limiting strategic weapons, if one is negotiated this year, can be regarded as spokesmen for or dupes of the munitions-makers; most are people persuaded that the Russians' intent is world conquest and that American security requires military supremacy. Adoption of the equal-rights amendment might in time cut into the profits of those who employ women at substandard wages, but this does little to account for the ferocity of those who are against it, most of whom begin their litany of opposition by saying that they, too, believe in equal pay for equal work. The economic consequences of providing public funds for elective abortions are negligible; indeed, the economy-minded might see such aid as a way of trimming expenses, since it would almost certainly lead to a decrease in the number of welfare recipients. But money and power have little to do with it; those who favor Medicaid assistance see it as a matter of fairness and decency, while those against it see it as a violation of moral and in some cases natural law.

In general, the interest groups that have been proliferating recently and that often seem to be dominating events

have as little to do with politics in the traditional sense as
they have to do with economic power or the struggle to attain
it. Though some groups find natural enemies on the right and
others on the left, they tend to be bipartisan, or nonpartisan,
and they tend to be more formidable as opponents of specific
measures or projects than as supporters. (Exceptions are some
of the environmentalist groups, such as Friends of the Earth,
Save the Whales, and the like.) Their force and cohesion stem
from their concentration on a single issue and the fact that
they do not brook division by linking that issue with others.
The right-to-life people take no position—though well they
might—on arms control, and their adversaries have no common view on deregulation of natural-gas prices or how to
combat unemployment and inflation. Those who opposed the
treaties with Panama are unlikely to be much concerned with
changes in the electoral process or with the plight of the
farmers. Although there has never been a time when voters,
as individuals, have felt strongly about more than two or
three of the dozens of issues on which the major parties, as
national coalitions and political brokerage houses, must take a
stand, the tendency today is to muster energy and resources
for a single, easily defined aim, such as curbing nuclear
power, fighting gun control, or reinstituting prayer in public
schools. Organizations like Americans for Democratic Action,
on the left, and the American Conservative Union, on the
right—both of which address themselves to a broad range of
foreign and domestic problems—are attracting less support
than those that focus on a single issue on which passions run
high and are undiluted by disagreement over other matters.
In 1977, Richard Viguerie, a publicist and entrepreneur of
pressure-bloc politics whose position on most questions is similar to that of the Republican Party, and who uses direct-mail
solicitation to organize interest groups on a bipartisan, issue-
by-issue basis, raised more than three times as much money as
the Republican National Committee, and his efforts seem to
have been correspondingly rewarded. This is a development
of considerable importance, and it helps to explain the peculiar political climate of the last two years. In many ways, the

President is both a beneficiary and a victim of the trend toward disintegration of the party system. He won nomination and election in a campaign that appealed to single-issue interests, and now that he must offer a more or less comprehensive and integrated program he is suffering at their hands. To be sure, some of his difficulties in rallying support in Congress are of his own making. He has not mastered the art of persuasion or the techniques of accommodation. Even so, given the kind of majorities the Democrats have in the House and Senate, he should be doing far better than he is, and he surely would be if the ground rules were not changing so rapidly and radically.

The decline of the party system began at least as far back as the thirties, when, under the New Deal, national issues began to supersede local and regional ones, and the central government replaced state and city organizations as dispenser of welfare and patronage. The growth of the central government was unaccompanied by structural changes to nationalize the parties in the way that other institutions were being nationalized. Mass communications advanced the process. Politicians found ways of building personal followings outside and largely independent of the regular organizations; audiences were assembled by radio and television networks rather than by local leaders. Party discipline became increasingly difficult to maintain. Even when they had majorities in Congress, Harry Truman and Dwight Eisenhower could not get the domestic legislation they sought, and John Kennedy's program succeeded only after he died and Lyndon Johnson, skilled at accommodation and consensus-building, took charge. Richard Nixon and Gerald Ford never had majorities. Vietnam led to widespread disaffection among Democrats, and Watergate among Republicans. Esteem for both the Presidency and Congress fell sharply, as did that for the parties, which were part of the machinery of deception. Candidates began playing down their party affiliations and, in some cases, deliberately distancing themselves from the organizations, as Carter did in the first part of 1977. (In statewide contests particularly, there is often no hint in the advertising as to which

party, if any, the office seeker represents.) Public financing
and enforced limits on campaign expenditures, though they
promote rectitude and discourage venality, restrict and
weaken the parties and almost force a candidate to seek support on an issue-by-issue basis. When the money came in
large sums from well-heeled donors, the clubhouses were still
effective instruments; they could not organize a movement,
but with the necessary funds they could get out the vote. Now
other organizations have that function. The civil-rights
groups mobilize the black vote. The trade unions, limited in
direct contributions, spend the money on political education
of their members and in getting them to the polls. Nonpartisan organizations like Common Cause and Public Citizen and
the National Rifle Association are in many places more effective than the local parties. And the finance committees,
which were never well served by the skills of district leaders,
must seek out donors of limited means and inevitably with
limited political concerns. The recent Supreme Court decision which holds that corporate contributions to political
causes are a right protected by the constitutional guarantee of
free speech (this would seem to revive the old controversy
over whether the corporation is or is not a human entity, with
all the rights and responsibilities of an individual) may negate
some of the laws on campaign financing, but since the majority opinion went no further than to authorize donations to influence the outcome of public referendums, it seems likely in
the short run to encourage the development of single-issue
politics.

The rise of single-issue interest groups is a reflection of the
growing complexity of American life and society, and particularly of the frustrations and impatience that this complexity
breeds. It is also a measure of a growing sophistication and a
heightened sense of political responsibility. It is almost impossible to imagine the long and divisive controversy over the
Panama Canal having taken place thirty or forty years ago.
Before the students in Panama began to riot fourteen years
ago, there were few Americans and few Panamanians who
questioned the propriety of our arrangements with the gov-

ernment in Panama City. Our maintenance of the waterway seemed a service to all nations, and our presence in the Canal Zone did not offend our anti-colonialist traditions, we were there not by conquest but by contract. Nor did it seem to offend—at least by comparison with today—the sensibilities of Panamanians, who were not yet caught up in the revolt against imperialism. But by 1964 the grievances the students expressed, if not their means of expression, seemed justified, and American opinion was ready for a generous redress; although the matters under negotiation were well known, there was little opposition to the efforts of the representatives of Presidents Johnson, Nixon, and Ford to conclude a treaty that would give full sovereignty to Panama over all the territories within its boundaries. It was not even an issue in Barry Goldwater's jingoistic campaign for the Presidency in the year negotiations got under way, and it might not have been an issue twelve years later if Ronald Reagan had not stumbled on it in New Hampshire—almost by accident, according to his strategist. But by then we had suffered defeat in Vietnam, and while this was accepted with better grace than had seemed likely a year or two earlier, there were millions who felt that the flag had been dishonored and who would feel further humiliated if we gave ground closer to home and yielded a strategic position that we ourselves had built. (In fact, the unskilled labor force was mostly West Indian. Our contribution was in financing, engineering, and defense. But, like the railroads and the interstate highways, it was a product of American enterprise.) At that, the issue may turn out this November to have been more contrived than genuine; it seems unlikely that the voters will punish candidates who are acceptable on bread-and-butter issues merely because of the possibility that certain difficulties will arise in Panama after 1999. It is possible, though, that despair over the ability of government to deal with bread-and-butter issues leads to a preoccupation with contrived ones.

Single-issue politics is a cause of frustration as well as a product of it. It is at least a partial explanation of why an unprecedented number of senior members of both houses of

Congress have decided not to seek reelection this year. Other causes are a desire to collect improved retirement benefits, to avoid the new requirements for disclosure of assets and income, and to make more outside money than is currently allowed. The work load is heavier than it used to be; last year, there were more than seven hundred recorded votes, as against approximately one hundred fifteen years ago. The post-Watergate reforms—many of them brought about by the zeal of Common Cause and other agitators for righteousness—have led to disclosure of political and moral as well as financial assets and liabilities. In the House, vote tellers now record how members vote not only on major bills but on amendments as well; it is no longer possible to conceal with the left hand what has been done by the right. But the most frequent complaint is that the mushrooming of interest groups has made the work of a legislator vastly more exasperating than it was a decade or so ago. No one knows how many of these groups are operating now or how great the recent increase has been—the register of lobbyists has always been an inadequate guide, because many of them do not register and many are only occasionally active—but it has been estimated that in the last few years more than two thousand new lobbies have come into existence. In the field of environment alone, there are hundreds, and merely to understand their complaints and demands requires that politicians develop expertise in the natural sciences and industrial technology. Matters that Congress was never called on to deal with in the past are now high on the agenda. Committees study drug abuse, child abuse, consumer abuse, the rights of women, the rights of the aging, and the rights of coyotes and wolves. It used to be that lobbyists could be dealt with on a simple, businesslike basis. If the deals they offered were unconscionable, they could be dismissed; if they were acceptable and promising, votes on the floor were bartered for votes at the polls, or the money to produce votes. But money—at least in large amounts from private sources—is no longer legal political tender, and votes must be garnered by appealing to constituencies that have little in common with one another and cannot be effectively organized by party machines.

In some ways, this seems a healthy development. There is a fragmentation of political interest, but most of the issues are genuine, and many of the new lobbies, very few of which are tainted by venality, represent legitimate public interests. The public the politicians deal with is far better educated than the one served when the parties controlled the process and dispensed the largesse that produced discipline, which is useful in an army but of questionable value in a deliberative body. There is no reason that those who make the laws of a nation should not be required to master its problems one at a time. Still, the party system has qualities that are seldom to be found in the interest groups. Henry Fairlie, a student of British institutions who is now examining American ones, has made a useful distinction between parties and movements. Political parties, he has written, produce political leaders; movements at their best produce educators and, sometimes, moral leaders. Parties exist to govern, and the major ones in most democracies are capable of governing; movements serve by influencing governments. Parties are instruments of compromise, which movements, as a rule, despise and consider corrupt—as often it is. Without compromise, though, there would be anarchy, and that is a condition which parties abhor and which, when they are strong and well led, they spare us.

THE POWER OF FETAL POLITICS[2]

The movement has many faces: from sweet ladies handing out red roses and right-to-life cookbooks, to demonstrators brandishing bottled fetuses and hoodlums attacking medical clinics. It has many voices as well: from righteous ministers preaching the sanctity of unborn souls, to editorials raising the specter of the holocaust, to crowds screaming "murderer" at elected officials who take a different position.

[2] Excerpted from magazine article by Roger M. Williams, senior editor. *Saturday Review.* 6:12–15. Je. 9, '79. © 1979 by Saturday Review Magazine Corp. All rights reserved. Reprinted by permission.

This is the anti-abortion movement, a cause that refuses to yield. Six years ago, the U.S. Supreme Court ruled that the right to have an abortion is beyond the reach of government. Since then, public-opinion polls have consistently shown that a majority of Americans favors making abortion a matter for patient and doctor to decide. Despite these developments, the subject is more politically explosive today than ever before. Opposition to abortion has become the most implacable, and perhaps the nastiest, public-issue campaign in at least a half century.

Anti-abortion forces are eagerly preparing for the elections of 1980 and beyond. U.S. Senators and Representatives, as well as many lesser officials, are being targeted for defeat. Even the forthcoming presidential race is within the movement's sights. "We hope to have at least one of the nominees on our side," says a national anti-abortion leader, "but in any case I assure you we'll have an impact."

Trumpeting their own future influence is part of the basic strategy of most political-pressure groups. But the anti-abortionists have demonstrated that they have muscles as well as mouths. In the 1978 elections they sent severe tremors through the political landscapes of such states as Minnesota and Iowa. In New York, running a gubernatorial candidate whose sole issue was opposition to abortion, they drew 132,-000 votes and secured for their Right to Life party an official place on the state ballot.

During the past 18 months, the movement has secured passage of abortion-restricting legislation in a dozen states and municipalities and laid the groundwork in a dozen others. Fourteen of the necessary 34 state legislatures have passed a call for a constitutional convention aimed at outlawing abortion. In addition, both houses of Congress are being bombarded with prospective constitutional amendments that would accomplish the same purpose. (Some versions make allowances for situations where the mother's life is threatened and for other so-called hard cases.)

Says former Iowa Senator Dick Clark, on whom the anti-abortionists successfully trained their fire last November:

"For candidates like me, with a clear-cut voting record on abortion, I see nothing but trouble ahead. The fact is that we're facing a small but very dedicated minority. A while back, I wouldn't have thought their constitutional amendment had a decent prospect. Now, I wouldn't underestimate its chances."

The gloom should not be spread too thick. It can be argued that, in their targeting of 1978 electoral candidates, the anti-abortionists lost as many battles as they won. Michigan Governor William Milliken was reelected despite having angered opponents of abortion by twice vetoing legislation that would have secured one of their principal goals—the elimination of government funding for the operation. In New Jersey, Illinois, and elsewhere, candidates running campaigns based on a right-to-life appeal were heavily outpolled.

Nonetheless, right-to-life successes are sufficiently numerous to demonstrate that the anti-abortion movement has become a significant political force. The question is, How long can it hope to remain one? What chances does it have of sustaining its bright blue flame of moral fury?

The war over abortion has an unusual history. Before the mid-1960s, opponents of abortion were in complete control. Then, within a six-year span, "pro-choice" activists—those who think abortion is a matter for the woman herself to decide—achieved a series of stunning successes: laws that legalized the practice in 18 states; court decisions invalidating prohibitive statutes in a half-dozen other states; and finally, in January 1973, the Supreme Court ruling that gave women an absolute right to have an abortion during the first three months of pregnancy and that severely limited state intervention through the sixth month.

Success, as it turned out, came too easily. The advocates of choice found themselves, like an armored column that has raced deep into enemy territory, outstripping their lines of supply. "The country wasn't with us at that point," concedes Karen Mulhauser, director of NARAL (National Abortion Rights Action League), the leading pro-choice organization. "Had we made more gains through the legislative and refer-

endum processes, and taken a little longer at it, the public
would have moved with us."

The Supreme Court decision spurred a number of statewide anti-abortion organizations into forming a National
Right to Life Committee (NRLC). Although a welter of other
groups is now at work on the issue, NRLC is the acknowledged kingpin. With chapters in all 50 states, it serves as the
movement's general lobbying office, clearing house, and strategy center. NRLC maintains especially close ties with the
Life Amendment Political Action Committee (LAPAC),
which is spearheading the campaign for a constitutional
amendment; their offices are located side by side in Washington's National Press Building; until recently, the two organizations were headed by a husband and wife—Judie (NRLC)
and Paul (LAPAC) Brown.

Paul Brown (Judie has retired) cheerfully describes himself as a political amateur, a status that always enhances the
image of pressure groups. Brown, 40, left a job as manager of
a K-Mart store to direct LAPAC. "For the first nine months,
the organization consisted of me," he says, "and for three of
those months I got no pay." NRLC and LAPAC raise money
without the services of professional, conservative-cause fund-
raisers; and, if one believes their figures, they spend it with
striking cost efficiency. According to the Federal Elections
Commission, LAPAC last year reported expenditures of $95,-
000, with a mere $7,000 of that split among eight candidates
who the committee was especially anxious to see win.
NRLC's own political-action committee reported no expenditures at all—a strange foundation for any sort of political
action.

At the state level, anti-abortion groups have been working
even greater apparent miracles. In Iowa, Senator Clark seems
to have been unseated for little more than would buy a new
car. In New York, the anti-abortion gubernatorial ticket spent
a mere $75,000, most of it for a final-week TV campaign. In
state after state, the anti-abortionists' reported expenditures
are almost trifling.

Big bangs for small bucks is only one of the surprises that

spring from the anti-abortion movement. Most of them involve impressive rationalizations on the part of people who
form the mainstay of the movement. It is curious, for example, that Americans who feel most threatened by minorities
and the poor are often the most determined to see that their
babies are born. The same people are usualy hostile to "big
government," yet they urge government at all levels to intervene in the personal lives of adult citizens. On a different
track, one finds Southern fundamentalist Protestants, who
once despised Roman Catholics only a little less than blacks,
now making common cause with Catholics on the abortion
issue.

The movement transcends these inconsistencies by means
of the extraordinary passion of the anti-abortion cause. While
right-to-life activity does draw strength from the fears and
phobias it holds in common with the New Right, it has a purpose and a life of its own. In our most recent broad-based social movements—civil rights, women's liberation, opposition
to the Vietnam War—only the extreme fringe has been un-
willing to compromise, to make gains piecemeal, to judge
candidates for office on some basis other than the movement's
own issue. Among anti-abortionists, however, everybody is
hardline. For them there is no give and take. A political candidate earns his tireless support or scathing opposition solely
by virtue of his position on abortion. (There are *some* limits.
When a Missouri Ku Klux Klansman ran for Congress on a
pro-life platform, reports a leader of NRLC, "we couldn't
support him.")

This singlemindedness—this "devotion," as its practition-
ers see it—gives rise to the charge that the anti-abortion
movement carries one-issue politics to the extreme. Missouri
Representative William Clay put the matter forcefully last
year when he told his congressional colleagues that, while he
personally doesn't believe in abortion, "I am sick and tired of
seeing [efforts to prohibit it] pop up on every piece of legislation. . . . It has become an albatross for all legislation, regardless of merit." Clay could have cited District of Columbia
statehood as a case in point. Last year *The Wanderer*, a na-

tional Catholic newspaper, urged the faithful to oppose
D.C.'s statehood on the ground that the new Congressmen
would be "virtually certain to be pro-abortion."

The anti-abortion retort amounts to a paraphrase of Barry
Goldwater's dictum about extremism and virtue; the defense
of life, they insist, transcends all other concerns. Furthermore, they say, many of the complainers were themselves
single-issue crusaders. "The black vote, Vietnam—those were
strictly one-issue," says LAPAC's Paul Brown. Playing a favorite trump card, he adds, "If you thought a candidate was
right on every issue but freedom of the press, would you vote
for him?"

Justification based on past movements is only partly con-
vincing. As MIT [Massachusetts Institute of Technology] political scientist Walter Dean Burnham says,

The right-to-lifers *are* doing what others have done, but with a
major difference in intensity. The emotional charge coming from
opposition to abortion is greater than from civil rights or the right
to bear arms or any similar cause. The people who are dedicated
right-to-lifers really believe that, in a special religious sense, they
are doing the Lord's work.

The effectiveness of the anti-abortion movement stems
largely from the wide front along which it attacks. From presidential campaigns to municipal ordinances, the movement
slugs away at one or another aspect of the issue. . . .

[But] despite its competitive advantages, the anti-abortion movement faces a very doubtful political future. Passing
a constitutional amendment is difficult at best and, as the
Equal Rights Amendment forces have learned, especially
hard when the campaign resembles a moral crusade. To be
politically powerful for more than a couple of years, the
movement must push aside a pair of time-tested American
propositions. One is that moral certainty and religious pre-
cepts seldom sustain political action. The other is that the
pluralistic character of our society has a way of fragmenting
the most passionate and seemingly unified causes.

A third, more speculative problem for the movement is

what Professor Burnham calls "our system-wide political and economic crisis." By that he means a general, long-term reordering of priorities in which issues like abortion will tend to get squeezed out by such overriding concerns as energy and inflation.

RENEGADE TAX REFORM: TURNING PROP 13 ON ITS HEAD[3]

In the year since Proposition 13 swept in from the West, the tax revolt has been seen almost exclusively as a conservative phenomenon: a rising tide of middle-class rage against four decades of New Deal, Fair Deal, and Great Society spending; a deliberate attack on the poor, the disadvantaged, the black and brown.

That perception is false—or so says the Ohio Public Interest Campaign (OPIC), the vanguard of a little-noticed but growing movement bent on turning the tax revolt on its head. Adamantly opposed to the cutbacks mandated by conservative tax-cut plans, OPIC believes the real target of taxpayers' anger is not government spending but the unfairness of the tax burden, the ability of large corporations and wealthy individuals to dodge through loopholes while the average citizen makes up the difference. And they plan to prove it with something called the Ohio Fair Tax Initiative, a measure that would cut taxes for low- and middle-income people but raise them for both the wealthy and big business.

Two states away, the Illinois Public Action Council—like OPIC a federation of citizens' groups, labor, and other organizations—is proposing similar legislation. "Our view is that tax reform is a progressive issue, not a right-wing issue," says Public Action director Bob Creamer. "People are mad about

[3] Excerpted from magazine article by David Osborne, free-lance writer. *Saturday Review.* 6:20-3. My. 12, '79. © 1979 by Saturday Review Magazine Corp. All rights reserved. Reprinted by permission.

their taxes, not about abstract spending questions. The issue is who pays."

In Massachusetts, too, a broad coalition of labor, citizens' groups, mayors, and the populist Mass Fair Share organization is pushing progressive tax reform. And elsewhere groups like Oregon Fair Share, People for Fair Taxes in Washington, and the Association of Community Organizations for Reform Now (ACORN), with chapters in 14 states, are watching closely. Nationally, the public-employee unions are joining the battle wherever it erupts, and the Progressive Alliance of left-wing Democrats put together by Douglas Fraser of the United Auto Workers (UAW) ranks tax reform at the top of its agenda.

"If we can succeed in Massachusetts, Illinois, and Ohio with substantial progressive tax reform," says Creamer, "then the odds are that we're going to see lots of other people trying it across the country, in the same way that the general tax limitation movement was so radically spurred by the victory [Howard] Jarvis and [Pau] Gann had in California [with Proposition 13]."

The progressive tax reform advocates point to the most detailed poll yet done on taxes, by Burns Roper, to support their contentions. "In the view of the American public," the poll concluded, "the major problem with the federal tax system in this country is its unfairness.... A growing majority sees middle-income people as overtaxed, while upper-income people and large businesses are seen as undertaxed." (The share of federal income-tax revenues borne by business has dropped over 5 percent in the last 10 years, with a parallel shift in the property-tax burden in many states.) Those interviewed by Roper ranked "tax reform" the nation's third most pressing problem, "lowering taxes" tenth. And 76 percent agreed that tax reform meant either "making taxes fairer to all" or "tightening up loopholes," while only 5 percent felt it meant their "taxes would probably go down."

The progressives also argue that Prop 13 proved itself a poor reflection of the nation's mood at the polls last November. "Jarvis got whipped," says Jim Savarese, director of public policy for the American Federation of State, County and Municipal Employees (AFSCME), a union that has made progressive tax reform its top priority. "There were only four states that had Prop 13-style things on the ballot—meat-ax approaches. The two that lost were in Oregon and Michigan, states that are substantial. The two that won were in Idaho and Nevada—and let's face it, they're no bellwethers of public opinion in the U.S."

If the new populists are correct—and can prove it at the polls—the impact on American politics will be tremendous. A tax revolt that has in one short year cut the very legs out from under big-spending liberalism will suddenly give rise to a new, anticorporate populism, challenging Democrats to redefine their politics not to the right, but to the left. A conflict that now pits middle-class taxpayers against welfare recipients will suddenly pit the average person against the wealthy and corporate elite.

"There's no way the old liberal approach—which is to continue to raise the taxes of the middle class and continue to spend money—can continue," explains Ira Arlook, director of OPIC.

Liberals will either have to give up on the social spending commitments that have made them liberals, or they'll have to become whatever we are—progressives, populists, whatever. It's very simple, but what makes it difficult for many people who want careers as politicians is that it puts them right up against the corporations, and that threatens their political careers. What we have to demonstrate is that people like us—who are an increasing majority and who can deliver on referenda and initiatives—threaten their careers even more.

As brash as such projections may seem, OPIC just may be the organization to pull them off. In four years of existence, its founders have assembled a remarkable coalition of labor, black, Hispanic, senior-citizen, church, neighborhood, and even small-business groups, and have almost single-handedly made the issue of tax breaks for business a major one in Ohio politics.

Ohio, overall, is a low-tax state. Personal and property taxes are very low, while business taxes fall in a middle range. In per capita spending on public services—schools, roads, police, and the like—the state ranks among the lowest in the nation. In fact, the real crisis in the state is not high taxes, as it was in California, but an inability to raise enough revenue to keep the public schools open. "If we're famous for anything in Ohio," says Arlook, "it's for our school closings."

So when cities like Cleveland offer highly profitable corporations like Sohio and National City Bank tax breaks worth close to a million dollars a year over 20 years—while schools are closing for lack of revenue—residents tend to swallow hard. OPIC took on the Cleveland city council over those two "abatements"—the official name for property-tax exemptions given corporations on new or redeveloped buildings—in 1977.

Arguing that such breaks make no difference in most corporate decisions to locate—and backed up by a series of national studies supporting their point—the organization made hay out of the issue. City council meetings were packed with angry citizens; demonstrations were held in which neighborhood residents mockingly dumped garbage from their streets on prime downtown construction sites classified as "blighted areas" under the state abatement laws; and hundreds of thousands of antiabatement leaflets were distributed.

By November of 1977 OPIC had made tax abatement a household word in Cleveland, one of two issues responsible for what the Cleveland *Plain Dealer* called "the greatest political purge in Cleveland's history," in which seven incumbent councilmen were defeated and outspoken populist Dennis Kucinich was swept into the mayor's office.

With the abatement issue igniting in other cities as well and California's Prop 13 looming on the horizon, the tax initiative was a natural. When the Jarvis-Gann landslide came in on June 7, says Arlook,

we decided we'd better jump out in front with a progressive tax-reform measure as quickly as possible, before we ended up having to fight a defensive battle against the Jarvis kind of approach. There are some other proposals in the wings, but by being first we have begun to define the terms of the debate in a way that's really crucial.

The Fair Tax Initiative combines two major elements: property-tax relief for low- and middle-income homeowners, renters, and farmers, and increased revenues for school funding generated by closing business-tax loopholes and making the personal and business income taxes more progressive. . . .

While the business community . . . [paints] the initiative as radical and dangerous, most legislators see it as a modest proposal, and if labor has a criticism—particularly public employees—it's that it doesn't go far enough.

If the proposal wins, says Mary Lynne Cappelletti, OPIC's lobbyist in the state capitol,

I think the national impact will be extraordinary. If we can win progressive tax reform in the bedrock heartland of the country, Ohio, with its diversity and its industrial base, then we really will have signaled the country that the taxpayers' revolt is a demand for progressive taxes. And that will be the clearest signal that's gone up since the lantern hung in Old North Church.

Such a signal—if indeed heard throughout the nation— would also have a direct impact on the current struggle at the heart of the Democratic Party. Should Ohio—and perhaps Illinois and Massachusetts as well—offer a reinterpretation of the tax revólt, liberal Democrats will again have some ground to stand on, some way to deliver tax relief to the hard-pressed middle and working classes without cutting back on spending for education, jobs, health, the cities, and the poor. They will have that ground, that is, *if* they are willing to slug it out with business. It's a big if, but as Jarvis and company have shown us, tax initiatives have a way of shaking things up—and quickly.

ACTIVIST NEIGHBORHOOD GROUPS[4]

A strong new political force—forged from the proliferating local activist organizations formed to stabilize and renew neighborhoods—has grown to maturity in America. Through recent victories in Washington and across the country, this lobby is replacing traditional institutions that have lost their vigor or their credibility.

For several years, many authorities were not sure whether the local groups, which began forming and multiplying a decade ago, would be a lasting phenomenon or a passing fad. But because they have thrived and grown under adversity and moved into new areas of activity, they are now generally considered to add an important new dimension to participatory democracy in this country.

At a time when government on all levels has been cutting back on social programs and innovations, the neighborhood activists—many of them perceived as radicals—have been winning legislative and policy battles against both city and Federal officials.

They have moved into a broad range of issues—health, education, voter registration and others—and they are originating and carrying out economic development and anticrime programs.

On the national level, the neighborhood lobby has succeeded in winning a series of laws and regulatory changes intended to combat what the activists view as the mindless ravages on residential areas of big government and big business.

In New York, Cleveland, Chicago and many other cities, coalitions of local groups have extracted policy changes from insurance and banking corporations and from government at various levels. In Texas, they are winning changes in state

[4] Excerpted from newspaper article "Activist Neighborhood Groups Are Becoming a New Political Force," by John Herbers, Washington-based national correspondent. New York *Times.* p A 1+. Je. 18, '79. © 1979 by The New York Times Company. Reprinted by permission.

housing laws that long favored landlords, allowing tenants to be evicted at will without a show of cause. In Pontiac, Mich., they blocked removal of a hospital to the suburbs. The list goes on.

Although urban decay continues, in many cities neighborhoods that five years ago seemed on the verge of abandonment are now well on the way to recovery, with much of the improvement due to the rise of local organizations.

Most of the organizations are self-financed, but in recent years they have been able to bypass state and local governments and obtain grants for specific purposes from the Federal Government.

Political Realignment Seen *

National Peoples Action, a coalition of 200 neighborhood groups across the country, started in Chicago in 1972 and is the movement's largest national forum. The coalition held its annual convention in Washington this weekend to celebrate its victories and map strategy for the 1980's.

Msgr. Geno Baroni, Assistant Secretary for the Office of Neighborhoods in the Department of Housing and Urban Development, and others view the movement as a major realignment of urban political forces.

In the past, he said, people in cities turned to the political machine, or to the church or civic groups, for social services and for redressing grievances. Now, the political parties are virtually powerless. Even in Chicago, where remnants of the Democratic machine of the late Mayor Richard J. Daley are still in place, ward leaders are unable to get much done for their neighborhoods. People have lost faith in government and other institutions, which have become so large and complex that they are unable to meet the needs of a diverse population.

"New York has not spent last year's Housing and Urban Development money," Monsignor Baroni said in an interview. "They just can't get it together. Twenty neighborhood groups have accomplished more in recent months than all of the Federal programs."

Diverse Reasons for Growth

Persons in the neighborhood movement interviewed in the past few weeks gave the following reasons for its growth at a time when the political tenor of the nation is basically conservative and change is difficult to achieve:

☐ Beyond their immediate goals, the groups are basically nonpartisan and nonideological. For example, they oppose redlining and other practices that have been used for discrimination, but they do so without raising the racial issue. Thus they have been able to bring together whites, blacks, other minority-group members and people of various ages without arousing antagonism.

☐ They have used direct action effectively—marches, sit-ins and other irritants aimed at government and corporate officials—but their leaders attribute their success more to extensive research and practices that have enabled them to document their grievances. In cluttered offices across the country—storefronts, warehouses, abandoned buildings—they are engaged in hard, gritty work that many people would find boring.

☐ By being small, unstructured and decentralized, they are in keeping with the times, which have seen a fragmentation of authority in institutions that held the country together for many decades. Every neighborhood is different, and the complexity and range of the organizations have permitted them to deal more specifically with needs than national or regional institutions could.

☐ After achieving the legislation they want, they pursue the agencies charged with administering it with dogged persistence. Two months ago, a coalition of groups in Brooklyn persuaded the Federal Deposit Insurance Corporation to deny a permit for a branch bank sought by the Greater New York Savings Bank because of noncompliance with the law against redlining, the practice of excluding certain areas from mortage lending, the first such denial in the country.

Strength in East and Midwest

Their names are a jungle of abbreviations and acronyms: AID (Against Investment Discrimination) in Brooklyn; N.W.B.C.C.C. (North West Bronx Community and Clergy Coalition); C.B.B.B. (Citizens to Bring Broadway Back) in Cleveland; ROBBED (Residents Organized for Better and Beautiful Environmental Development) in San Antonio; PAR (Playland Area Residence) in Council Bluffs, Iowa,; UWE-COACT (United West End-Citizens Organization Acting Together) in Duluth, Minn., and so on.

The organizations are in various stages of development. Those in the large cities of the East and Middle West are the most sophisticated. The movement has spread more recently in the Southwest and West.

The Bois d'Arc Patriots of Dallas offer a typical example. The Patriots took their name from the bois d'arc tree, whose hard wood was used in the foundation for many of the old plantation-style houses that still stand in East Dallas. The neighborhood, close to the business district, had become largely a slum by 1972 when a young man named Charlie Young moved there from Grapevine, Tex.

The old houses had been turned into multiple-family apartments, most of them overrun with rats and cockroaches. Mr. Young, who lived in one of the apartments, went to the landlady with other tenants and proposed a tenant-landlord effort for extermination.

Winning Rights for Tenants

"She just laughed at me," Mr. Young said. . . . He began organizing the tenants and affiliated with the Patriots, who were working in several Dallas neighborhoods. They succeeded in establishing, through law and practice, some basic rights for tenants and moved on to other issues.

Two years ago, the Patriots went to City Hall to protest what they viewed as the failure of the city government to give East Dallas its fair share of Federal Community Development funds. They took a model of an East Dallas house. At the end of their presentation they dramatically smashed the house and out ran thousands of cockroaches, which soon spread throughout the council chambers.

After that everyone in Dallas knew who the Bois d'Arc Patriots were. Because of the city's long tradition of paternalism, City Hall and the business establishment had provided them with a perennial target. They have moved into a multitude of issues: For example, they are now fighting to get a federally financed health clinic in East Dallas so residents will not have to go across town to Parkland Hospital. They publish a newspaper, "The Peoples Voice," run a community school and sponsor neighborhood suppers.

Elderly Among the Most Militant

They have no members, only participants, said Mr. Young, who is the Patriots' spokesman. Some of the most militant participants are elderly people who have lived in the neighborhood for many years. Patriots recently received a $90,000 grant from the Law Enforcement Assistance Administration in Washington to run a crime-control program, a grant that was bitterly opposed by state and city officials on the ground that it usurped the authority of the Dallas police. The money, however, is being used for a youth center, education and transportation for elderly through unsafe streets.

By and large, East Dallas is now a pleasant neighborhood of large and small homes, one-third white, one-third black and one-third Mexican-American. Many of the old ones are being restored by young couples who generally join a neighborhood organization. Others are being restored by speculators who are viewed as a threat to the neighborhood because of displacement of the poor.

The Patriots, Mr. Young said, are wary of joining national or regional coalitions for fear they would lose their grass-roots flavor. "Our strength is in the people of this neighborhood," he said, "and we don't want to lose that."

Viewing Washington as Threat

The neighborhood groups in Northern cities almost immediately moved into the national arena because they saw the Federal Government more of a threat to their neighborhoods than City Hall. They were instrumental in winning the 1975 antiredlining law in the Community Redevelopment Act of last year. It requires regulated financial institutions to make a conscious effort to put money back into low- and moderate-income areas they serve.

The groups affiliated with National Peoples Action are now seeking through law and through confrontations with corporations to make home insurance premiums in the central cities equitable with those elsewhere.

Their national lobbying effort resulted in the appointment of a Presidential commission on neighborhoods, which issued a 1,000-page report a few weeks ago with a mind-boggling list of recommendations for government action.

"We were criticized for not recommending some big national program," said Gail Cincotta of Chicago, chairman of National Peoples Action and a member of the commission. "We don't want any more big government programs. It was big government programs that destroyed our cities. But we are dealing with a lot of very complex issues and there are a lot of things the Government can do even if they are not dramatic."

Partisan Political Role Rejected

With hundreds of highly organized neighborhood groups in place across the country, the question has been raised as to whether they could not be used to promote the election of a Presidential candidate, as Democratic Party organizations did for many years.

Most leaders are quick to reject this idea, for the same reason that Mr. Young was wary of national coalitions. They prefer to present their goal to the candidates of both parties and avoid becoming identified with any party or personality. Whoever holds office, despite campaign promises, is usually considered the enemy because the groups organize chiefly against big, insensitive bureaucracy, not particular officials.

"If we endorse someone we would feel compromised once he got in," said Mrs. Cincotta. "We just take them on as they come up, Democrats or Republicans."

GAYS IN THE STREETS[5]

San Francisco. Have three facts to relate: 1) On November 27, 1978, Dan White, former policeman, fireman and supervisor, shot and killed the mayor of San Francisco, George Moscone, and another member of the Board of Supervisors, Harvey Milk, the city's first avowedly homosexual elected official. White had been angered at Moscone's refusal, supported by Milk, to reappoint him to the board after he had resigned, two weeks earlier, in a moment of despair. 2) On May 21 a jury found White guilty of voluntary manslaughter. Most observers had anticipated a verdict of first- or second-degree murder. 3) That evening thousands of gay people in San Francisco rioted. Hundreds of windows were shattered, at least 12 squad cars were burned and dozens of police and protesters were injured.

The last development is for me by far the most interesting. The riot marks a significant moment in the evolution of political awareness among homosexuals. On the surface it lacks the characteristics that most Americans associate with politics. But its inspiration was profoundly political, and it can be dis-

[5] Reprint of magazine article by Paul Robinson, contributing editor. *New Republic.* 180:9–10. Je. 9, '79. Reprinted by permission of THE NEW REPUBLIC, © 1979 The New Republic, Inc.

tinguished from earlier violent incidents involving homosexuals precisely because of its political nature.

Of course San Francisco should not be confused with the rest of the country. In fact one must even distinguish among various parts of San Francisco itself. The city, so far as I know, is like no other in terms of the circumstances of its homosexual population. Most important is the sheer number of avowed homosexuals. Nobody knows exactly how many there are, but the figures usually cited range from 50,000 to 100,-000—in a city with a total population of less than 750,000. In short, gays represent a significant constituency in San Francisco, which means that at election time politicians feel obliged to pay court to them, to develop special appeals, to create (if you're cynical) a distinctive set of fibs, since one cannot hope to win the gay vote with the usual generalized mendacity.

Gays are also a large and visible element in the city's economy. There are gay parts of town, places where many businesses are run by and cater to gays. One particular neighborhood known as the Castro, which provided most of the troops for the May 21 protest, is owned and populated largely by gays. It is sometimes called a gay ghetto—not in the sense of a "black ghetto" or the "Warsaw ghetto" (which implies poverty and enforced isolation), but more like a university town's "faculty ghetto": a homogeneous and somewhat exclusive population, with a certain uniformity of manners and opinion. Many people, including some gays, complain about this ghetto existence. But they fail, I think, to recognize the political advantages of such physical proximity, which might be compared to the proximity of workers in a 19th-century factory, a development that Marx considered a necessary prelude to the creation of proletarian class consciousness. The ability to think and act politically often depends on such humdrum material realities. In the Castro one can elicit a large and rapid response simply by persuading everybody who lives there to step outside his or her door, or to step outside one of the many gay bars in the neighborhood. This was demonstrated only a few weeks ago when police tried to stop someone from putting up a poster, leading to the sudden appearance of a mass of angry gays in the streets. The situation is comparable to that of blacks in Watts [in Los Angeles] or Bedford-Stuyvesant [in Brooklyn].

So San Francisco is exceptional. It is exceptional, however, in the sense of being in the vanguard, not of being a mere fluke. Many sexual studies suggest that the gay population of the country is enormous: the figure one reads most often, based on the Kinsey reports (and arguably exaggerated), is 10 percent, which means over 20 million individuals. Thus good biological (or characterological) grounds exist for contending that San Francisco is unique only in being the sole city in the country, perhaps in the world, where the reality of human sexual orientation is objectively reflected. If this is indeed the case, what happens to the gay population of San Francisco is of more than local interest. It is a portent of what awaits the nation as a whole.

The May 21 riot was political in two senses: first, it explicitly addressed the issue of justice, which, if we follow Plato, is the most fundamental category of political analysis. The crowd at City Hall shouted repeatedly, "We want justice." Second, it required abstraction. The individuals who rioted, unlike those who protested police harassment at the Stonewall, a gay bar in New York City, 10 years ago, did not themselves face any immediate or tangible imposition. They had to think abstractly, indeed almost technically, to get from a verdict of voluntary manslaughter to their act of civil disobedience. Reasoning of this sort presumes that a significant group in the population has become aware not merely of its own existence, but also of its rights and power. The riot, I can't help feeling, marks a kind of political coming of age for homosexuals in San Francisco and, vicariously, throughout the country. If one is a liberal, one hopes that this political consciousness will eventually find less costly forms of expression (as it did, for instance, the following evening, when a crowd of 4000 peacefully celebrated Harvey Milk's birthday). But it would be unhistorical to bemoan the protesters' resort to violence or their insistence on seeing the case in terms of sexual preju-

dice, instead of simple injustice. Movements of social liberation just don't happen that way, much as we might wish they
did. There is, then, cause for celebration in this collective
emergence of gays from the political closet. I, at least, found
it enormously moving.

The Dan White case is less interesting for what it reveals
about the attitudes of heterosexuals. It merely confirms the
existence of a prejudice that one already knew existed,
whether one chooses to stress White himself, his jurors or the
police who responded to the protesters with such remarkable
vehemence. Still, in all humanity, one shouldn't forget the
profound anxiety caused by the rise of militant homosexuality. Deeply felt prejudice is still prejudice, but the sources of
homophobia are more inaccessible than the facile bigotry
that serves to rationalize economic interest. Sexual identity is
a painful and irrational matter. It touches a perennial aspect
of every individual's experience. Psychologically speaking, it
is easier to overcome racism—difficult though that may be—
than to exterminate feelings about the wrongness of sexual
acts between persons of the same sex. If our sexual lives were
as manageable as our economic lives (that is, just barely), we
might more reasonably call White, his jurors, or the San Francisco police "fascists." But at this stage in man's psychological
evolution, such language is overblown.

One final matter: White's jurors should be allowed the
possibility of error. From everything I've read, White seems
to be a reactionary homophobe who acted with sufficient
self-possession to justify a verdict of second-degree murder, at
the least. But juries make mistakes, even when no ideological
questions are involved. Jurors are amateurs trying to do a job
that, because of its complexity, in reality requires professionals. They must cope with an arcane body of law, with
large amounts of conflicting evidence and argument, and, finally, with their own emotions. Under the circumstances, the
wonder is that justice is ever served. In this particular case,
moreover, the prosecution was embarrassingly feeble, above
all in its failure to address the political nature of the slayings.

We retain the jury system because it has compensating

virtues, above all, I believe, the one identified by Alexis de Tocqueville: jury duty (or even the possibility of it) is an exercise in political responsibility, thus in democracy. We tolerate the system's sometimes awesome inefficiency because of its importance, in a more general way, to the well-being of our society.

Like last year's legislative struggle over gay rights, the Dan White affair has served, paradoxically, as a vehicle for homosexual liberation. One should merely avoid underestimating the intellectual and, above all, psychological difficulties that liberation poses for heterosexuals.

THE ANGRY WEST VS. THE REST[6]

More and more, Westerners complain that a powerful absentee landlord, the Federal government, is regulating them to death; that a Congress dominated by Eastern interests is riding roughshod over their views on land and water; and that Jimmy Carter's new energy policies threaten to replay the rape of the old frontier. And with tempers ragged all around, the West is spoiling to fight back. "A new Mason-Dixon line is being drawn at the 100th meridian," warns Colorado's Gov. Richard D. Lamm. "Regional politics are greater than at any time since the Civil War."

The 100th meridian is where the West begins. Knifing down from the Dakotas, it slices just east of Dodge City, Kans., clips the Oklahoma panhandle, and cuts through Texas, marking off a thirteen-state area with 39 million people that is rapidly becoming a region apart. To the west of this climatological and soil barrier, most of the land is owned by the Federal government and agriculture is largely impossible without massive irrigation; but the same arid lands have

[6] Excerpted from magazine cover story by Tom Mathews, senior writer, *Newsweek;* with Gerald C. Lubenow, San Francisco bureau; Martin Kasindorf, Los Angeles bureau; and Gloria Borger, Washington bureau. *Newsweek.* 94:31–4+. S. 17, '79. Copyright 1979, by Newsweek, Inc. All Rights Reserved. Reprinted by Permission.

vast deposits of low-sulfur coal in accessible veins, heavy crude oil, mountains of oil shale and plenty of uranium. And just as the nation most sorely needs the West's bountiful resources and goodwill, a palpable sense of being wronged seems to be turning Westerners inward. "It's the West against the rest," says Jerry Norris of the western office of the Council of State Governments. "The West has become what the South was in the '40s and '50s."

Battles: The West's tradition of hostility to Big Government and cantankerous dealings with outsiders goes back as far as its great nineteenth-century battles over railroad routes and rates, protective tariffs and free silver. But the new strain of sectionalism seems more potent than anything since the Great Depression swept away many of the country's local differences in a wave of mutual hard times. Regional strains sprouted over the last decade, but they were overshadowed by such national issues as Vietnam and Watergate. Now they are out in the open. "What we are seeing is a revival of regionalism, a return to the old pattern of American politics," says political scientist Seymour Martin Lipset of Stanford University. And the revival promises to test Federal-state relations, the effectiveness of Congress and the operations of the White House.

One measure of the anger now firing up the West is the way it has united an otherwise maverick group of states and rugged individualists with a new sense of common cause—and a conviction that the rest of the country doesn't share, understand or sympathize with the region's most vital concerns. Part of the trouble is simply that the West *is* different. Issues vital to the West—such as scarce water, government-owned land or illegal aliens from Mexico—matter very little in New York or Ohio. And while the politically powerful industrial states in the East and Midwest are struggling to stem decay—mainly urban blight and aging industries—the West is preoccupied with problems of growth: exploiting its mineral wealth while protecting its environmental richness, ensuring vital water supplies and balancing a changing agricultural economy with a post-industrial boom. "We rec-

ognize the problem," says Oregon's Gov. Victor Atiyeh. "The
West needs to build and the East needs to rebuild."

Rifts: Even where East and West share the same problems, the solutions often cause regional rifts. Strip-mining
regulations tailored for Appalachia don't fit conditions in the
Rockies. Housing formulas designed for the crowded ghettos
of Newark, Harlem or Chicago's South Side square badly with
the needs of sprawling newer cities like Phoenix. Energy-al-
location schemes to refine more heating oil for New England
mean less gasoline for the car-dependent West. And the 55-
mile-an-hour speed limit, generally accepted in the East, galls
Westerners facing 100-mile straightaways. . . .

Get-up-and-go: The steady westward drift of the population has provided the West with its most important resource—people. Though Western states (except California)
are still sparsely populated, they are growing more than twice
as fast as the nation as a whole. In the past decade, Alaska's
population has swelled by more than one-third, Nevada's by
30 per cent, Wyoming's by nearly one-quarter and Utah's by
20 per cent. "The population in places of pervasive decline
like New York and Ohio tends to be less mobile, older and less
ambitious," says demographer Peter Morrison of the Rand
Corp., who finds Westerners have more get-up-and-go.

The West has also become a state of mind as well as a
stretch of territory. New Westerners tend to characterize
themselves as self-sufficient, open, friendly and tolerant of differences. "You're considered a good guy until you prove otherwise; in the East it's the other way around," says William
Smallwood, education consultant in Sun Valley, Idaho. Such
attitudes ease the way for transplanted Easterners. . . .

Many political leaders in the West now argue for a step-
by-step approach to the energy crisis, one that emphasizes
conservation and provides enough water for agriculture. To
defray the costs of becoming the country's energy field, Western states now demand Federal impact assistance for communities that must cope with the problems of quick growth and
the threat of quick decline. Montana has set stiff coal severance taxes designed to make those who benefit most from

Montana coal pay for the side effects of mining it. "We will determine at what pace development will proceed, where plants will be located, how water will be allocated, and the impact will be shared by all Americans," says Governor [Thomas L.] Judge of Montana. "If the East refused to pay the severance tax, uphold our environmental regulations and provide impact aid, it would mean war—but I don't think you'll see that."

The long and short: If the West's destiny isn't altogether manifest, its new determination is absolutely clear. "In the 1960s, when the Federal government wanted to do anything, states rolled over and played dead; that's over as far as we're concerned," says Utah's Governor [Scott M.] Matheson. Optimists predict the region's growing population will ultimately give it the political power it now lacks in Congress. Pessimists, studying the water table, believe that the population must level off, leaving the West where it has always been: long on resources, short on capital and outvoted in Washington.

Under the circumstances, the West is likely to stay angry for a long time. If passions are to subside and the interests of the nation to be adjusted with those of the region, the East will have to acknowledge that the West has come of age. But a heavy responsibility will also fall upon the West to define its own trade-offs—between growth and environmental quality and between states' rights and Federal subsidy. "We are going to have to be a region with synfuel plants and wilderness areas side by side," says Governor Lamm of Colorado. "Our streams must support fish and wildlife, agriculture and industry. It's going to require a good deal of creative planning to bring about that balance and harmony. The jury is out on whether we can achieve it." How long the jury can stay out is a troubling question, for the frontier is a thing of the past, and an energy-hungry country no longer has time on its side.

IV. REACHING THE VOTERS

EDITOR'S INTRODUCTION

The invention of radio radically altered the world of American politics. Its instantaneous dissemination of political messages unified the consciousness of the American people in a way that newspapers never could. At the same time, it also decreased direct social interaction between voters and candidates (a trend accelerated by television). Candidates could more easily talk to greater numbers of people through the electronic media than they ever could through tours and personal appearances. Consequently, the latter activities have greatly decreased. Today, when they do occur, they are almost always events staged for the benefit of the broadcast media.

It can be argued that this decrease in direct social interaction was the groundwork for the alienated single-issue politics that is on the rise today. Electronic media may speed the flow of information, but they also simplify the transmitted information and also encourage feelings of distance and powerlessness in their audiences. How such feelings may be counteracted (or exploited, depending upon one's point of view) is analyzed in this section.

The first article, by Nick Kotz, the Pulitzer prizewinning author of *A Passion for Equality,* is an extract from an *Atlantic* profile of Richard Viguerie. Viguerie is an extraordinarily successful direct-mail fund raiser who devotes himself to right-wing causes. His computerized mailing operation brings in large amounts of money and has given hard-line conservatives strong support in political contests across the country. Kotz points out that operations like Viguerie's, given the political apathy of most Americans, "permit the [political] arena to be dominated by small, intensely partisan splinter groups."

Michele Willens, reporting for *Politics Today*, describes next how entertainers have assumed an important role in candidates' fund-raising plans. The law restricts contributions by individuals to $1,000, but entertainers can donate the entire net revenue of a performance to a candidate or cause. The presence of star entertainers in a campaign, moreover, assures media attention and coverage for politicians who might otherwise go unnoticed.

In the third article in this section, taken from the *Atlantic*, André Mayer, a historian, and Michael Wheeler, an instructor at the New England School of Law, examine the growing trend toward the use of an old political device, the referendum. Issues like California's Proposition 13, which cut state property taxes drastically, are finding their way onto more referendum ballots than in the past. Although voters think that legislation through referenda gives them a strong voice in policy making, in reality, say Mayer and Wheeler, the propositions, and the interest groups backing them, often take advantage of "voter ignorance and . . . [make] use of modern publicity techniques to confuse instead of enlighten."

Michael Nelson, a political scientist, takes a more optimistic view of "the politics of direct action"; discussing the rising use of the initiative in a *Saturday Review* article, he declares that "support for the initiative . . . may prove a constructive way of tapping the public's dissatisfaction."

Another political scientist, Ben Martin, examines in a *Harper's* article the movement to rewrite the Constitution, arguing that such an action would create a more up-to-date document, better able to cope with modern political developments.

The book concludes with observations by Christopher Buchanan, a staff member of the *Congressional Quarterly Weekly Report*, on "party-crashers"—outsiders, often novices to politics, who capture party nominations even though they have never actively engaged in party politics before. According to Buchanan, it is money that turns the trick (an ominous note that harks back to Arthur Schlesinger's warning about the flow of political power in the future). "Money, either

from a candidate's pocket or from special interest groups,"
writes Buchanan, "has always been the single most important
explanation for the success of candidates with little party
backing or public recognition."

KING MIDAS OF "THE NEW RIGHT"[1]

The computer room, ninety feet long, is in an ordinary
white brick office building in Falls Church, Virginia, a
sprawling suburb of Washington, where the Richard A. Viguerie Co. rents three floors. It is guarded by two different security systems, and the programmer on duty opens the door
to Richard Art Viguerie himself only when he produces
proper identification. Inside are two giant IBM computers,
two high-speed printers, and ten tape units. In an adjoining
room, protected by even more elaborate security precautions,
are stored 3000 rolls of magnetic tape. On the tapes are en-
coded the names of 15 million people and vital information
about them. Richard Viguerie points to the round cans holding the tapes and grins. "If you're a conservative, your name
should be in there somewhere," he says.

If you have been the recipient recently of unsolicited mail
asking for money to help fight the Panama Canal treaty, abortion, gun control, school busing, labor law reform, or the
Equal Rights Amendment, chances are your name is recorded
in Viguerie's computers. If you were asked to support Senators Jesse Helms (R-N.C.) and Strom Thurmond (R-S.C.), or, a
few years back, George Wallace for President, the letters
came from Viguerie's operation. Viguerie's biggest clients
today are a band of right-wing groups that includes the Conservative Caucus, the Gun Owners of America, the Committee for the Survival of a Free Congress, the National

[1] Excerpted from magazine article by Nick Kotz, author of several books and re-
cipient of Pulitzer Prize for reporting of the national scene. *Atlantic.* 242:52-3+. N. '78.
Reprinted by permission of The Sterling Lord Agency, Inc. Copyright © 1978 by Nick
Kotz.

Conservative Political Action Committee (NCPAC), and Americans Against Union Control of Government. They were virtually created by Viguerie and his genius for fund-raising. This year alone he will raise an estimated $15 million for his clients, money they will use to lobby against liberal legislation and to organize conservative voting groups. Perhaps most important, they will pour money and political soldiers into the campaigns of conservative candidates.

The reform of the federal campaign spending laws in 1974 meant that a Howard Hughes, a Clement Stone, or a Stewart Mott could no longer bankroll a candidate almost singlehandedly. The law now limits personal contributions to $1000 per candidate. For presidential candidates, federal subsidies help to fill the coffers, and spending limits keep costs under control, but members of Congress have been deprived of their fat cats and have received nothing in return.

As things have turned out, though, many congressional candidates didn't really need to worry. Campaign treasuries for the 1978 elections have been rapidly replenished by the enormously effective use of an unobtrusive technique whose success could have profound implications for the political scene.

The fund-raising technique is direct mail, and the new contributors are the hundreds of thousands of Americans who send $10, $15, or $25 in response to mail solicitations—computerized letters with a simulated personal touch. The Republican party has caught on to direct mail much faster than the Democrats. In a reversal of past giving habits, more than one million small donors now support the party of big business, while the Democrats still depend on wealthy big contributors. But other important beneficiaries of the direct mail fund-raising boom are the militantly conservative political organizations, causes, and candidates loosely called, for want of a better term, "the New Right."

The direct mail phenomenon has also spawned a new breed of fund-raiser. These political direct mail fund-raisers are generally inconspicuous men in Washington: Roger Craver, who engineered Common Cause's mail success, and has now been hired to help the Democratic party find the "little people"; Wyatt Stewart and Stephen Winchell, who pioneered in GOP mail fund-raising. But Richard Viguerie is both conspicuous and controversial. At forty-five, he has become a multimillionaire through computerized mailings. He is not just a fund-raiser but a powerful influence within the New Right.

"The conservative movement has always been good at producing writers and debaters," says Viguerie, "but it never had anybody who knew how to market ideas to the masses. Well, that's what I am doing."

Viguerie's dream—and the nightmare of his antagonists, who include liberals and mainstream Republican leaders—is that the New Right will fuse a conservative majority from the disparate grievances of angry citizens who are exercised over gun control, abortion, homosexuality, drugs, unions, disarmament, and taxes. He describes his job as "organizing discontent," providing the postage stamps for those citizens who want to "send them a message." Moderate Republicans who go against the conservative orthodoxy have received the message: the New Right . . . [in 1978] helped to defeat four-term Senator Clifford Case in the primaries in New Jersey, and challenged other Republican liberals and moderates in Illinois, California, Iowa, and Massachusetts.

Viguerie and the political action committees he has created wield a considerable amount of unchecked power. Acting in concerted fashion, they can pour significant amounts of money into launching a candidate. (Each committee can legally contribute $5000.) They can flood the country with mail on an issue, stirring up a mountain of protest letters to Congress or the White House. Viguerie's power stems from his ownership and control of the largest and most effective mailing list of Americans who will actively support conservative causes. . . .

Direct mail advertising, at least as old as the 1872 Montgomery Ward catalogue, is today a $6-billion-a-year business, selling more than $60 billion worth of goods and services. Charities raise $10 billion a year through the mail; $500 million of that goes to the mailing consultants. Politicians have asked for money through the mail for years, but on a small scale until George McGovern, cut off from the traditional big contributors, raised $20 million by mail in 1972. Viguerie raised $7 million for Wallace. And this year candidates and committees will have taken in more than $100 million via the mails.

It is, however, an expensive advertising medium, and so it is crucial that it be aimed accurately at the most receptive audience. A letter asking for money to defeat a candidate who favors gun control legislation ideally should go only to rabid antilegislation gun owners; voters in favor of gun control, who would be enraged by the letter, should not see it or even have any idea that it's being sent.

"The interesting thing about direct mail," says Viguerie, "is that when it's professionally done, it has a devastating impact. It's like using a water moccasin for a watchdog—it's very quiet."

Viguerie's computer room in Falls Church is very quiet too. His 30 million names represent no more than 15 million people, once duplications are eliminated, but among these is a hard core of 4 million conservative activists, and the power of Viguerie and his clients rests on those 4 million—an enormous number of people in light of the political inertia of the American public. For access to this list, one must go to Richard Viguerie.

There are also about 4 or 5 million activists at the other end of the political spectrum. But no single fund-raiser commands their names, and after years of writing generous checks for civil rights, ending the war in Vietnam, impeaching Richard Nixon, and saving the whales and the redwoods, the liberal activists are sluggish.

The words "New Right" have been used in a variety of conservative contexts. At its broadest, the term describes the renewed conservative activism in the country during the last few years. At its narrowest, some veteran conservatives have commented sardonically, the New Right is nothing more than Richard Viguerie and his clients. The term has been used to

differentiate between older conservative groups, such as the
American Conservative Union (founded in 1964), which concentrates on economic issues, and newer groups, which have
focused on social, or "pro-family," issues such as homosexuality, school busing, abortion, and drugs.

What is "new" about the New Right, most conservatives
would agree, is pragmatism. The new organization is reflected in the weekly strategy sessions, held over drinks and a
light dinner, in the conference room of Viguerie's office.
There are staff from the Senate Steering Committee and the
House Research Group, new alliances of conservative Republicans; members of older conservative groups such as the National Right to Work Committee and the American
Conservative Union; and the leaders of the new groups that
Viguerie's fund-raising has spawned.

The conservative activists debate which congressional
candidates to support and plan common strategy on legislative issues. They take some of the credit in the present Congress for defeating common situs picketing, labor law reform,
a consumer protection agency, and federal financing of congressional elections, and claim a major role in defeating postcard voter registration, an issue the Republican leadership
thought too popular to oppose. Even their loss on the Panama
Canal had some pluses, they feel. Hundreds of thousands of
conservatives were identified, and new resources were
discovered.

Viguerie and his coterie distinguish between conservative
"spokesmen"—such as Ronald Reagan or Barry Goldwater—
and actual "leaders"—in which role they cast themselves.
"The difference," says Viguerie, "is that spokesmen make
speeches, and leaders make things happen." If Reagan had
been a leader rather than just a spokesman, Viguerie believes,
the Panama Canal treaty would have been defeated.

Among elected officeholders viewed by Viguerie as "leaders" are Senators Hatch (R-Utah), Helms (R-N.C.), and Paul
Laxalt (R-Nev.), and Representative Philip Crane (R-Ill.),
whom Viguerie envisions as the conservative choice for President in 1980. Viguerie's ideas about his own leadership are

not taken seriously by all conservative officeholders. Laxalt, for example, sees Viguerie as "the best direct mail mechanic in the business," but not as a leader.

Among his New Right colleagues, Viguerie is respected for his integrity. But other conservatives see him as an opportunistic businessman who has exploited the conservative movement for maximum profit. Their complaints usually have to do with the amount of money that goes to fund-raising costs rather than to candidates. Wyatt Stewart, a former Viguerie employee who now raises money for the Republican Congressional Campaign Committee, says that Viguerie's costs are much too high. Stewart has raised about $8 million a year for the GOP committee through direct mail at a cost of $2 million, or 25 percent. Viguerie's fund-raising costs for New Right groups have averaged about 50 percent of the proceeds. But Viguerie's clients say they are not unhappy. "We probably could get someone cheaper, but Richard can get the job done when you need it done," said Paul Weyrich of the Committee for Survival of a Free Congress.

Viguerie has ready answers to the criticism of his high costs. Initial prospecting for a new organization or a new candidate may be very expensive, he says, but costs drop dramatically as mailings yield renewed contributions. Like capital expenditures in business, he says, these costs can be viewed fairly only by amortizing them over a period of years.

Even when costs run as high as 100 percent of funds raised, as in an unsuccessful conservative campaign to defeat Senator Jacob Javits (R-N.Y.), Viguerie has an explanation.

The purpose of our mail isn't just to raise funds. We are building a movement. Direct mail is a way to get people involved, to educate them, to turn out the vote. Direct mail is a form of advertising and conservatives have found it a way to communicate with our people and to pay for the communication. What are the critics suggesting? That we raise money by direct mail and then spend it on television?

Viguerie's associates and employees respect the consistent values they find in his business and family life and his political beliefs. "I'd be shocked if Richard ever took a project to make money that hurt the conservative cause," said Terry Dolan, the NCPAC chairman. "He is one businessman who won't do anything that counters his principles."

Yet there runs through his professional career a stream of complaints about his fund-raising practices. His direct mail business has specialized in philanthropy as well as politics, and his work for charitable causes has drawn many objections from state officials and Better Business Bureaus—the essential charge is that too much of the money raised goes back to Viguerie. New York State took action in 1973 against Citizens for Decent Literature, an antipornography group, on grounds that 93 percent of funds raised went to Viguerie. In 1977, New York State banned solicitations by the Korean Cultural and Freedom Foundation after discovering that of the $1.5 million it raised in 1975 to help hungry children, less than $100,000 went to the children and more than $900,000 was paid to the Viguerie firm. (The rest went to administrative and other expenses.)

The Council of Better Business Bureaus' Philanthropic Advisory Service has a thick file on Viguerie's charity projects, including a recent complaint concerning Bibles for the World. This group seeks to give a Bible to everyone in the world listed in a telephone directory, but in its first year it raised $802,028 from Viguerie's direct mail at a total fund-raising cost of $899,255.

Viguerie's defense, again, is that initial costs are enormous. Nevertheless, contributors don't realize that their money is often used to build a bigger and better contributor list.

Viguerie's book company, Prospect House, gives away "conservative book packs" to students, ministers, and veterans. Direct mail appeals to names on his various lists ask for donations to subsidize these book gifts. This is in fact purely a business venture, and the Council of Better Business Bureaus worries that the mail solicitations look as though they are nonprofit or charitable. These appeals utilize the letterhead of some worthy cause. One solicitation, under the letterhead "Help Our Police," featured a picture of a policeman being beaten by an antiwar demonstrator. Funds contributed would be used to provide a newsletter for policemen, alerting them to dangerous radicals. Viguerie insists that his letters make clear that they are business ventures and at some point in the letters Prospect House is mentioned. By his own advertisements, Prospect House has received at least $2.7 million in "contributions" from 165,000 "donors."

It is too early to predict whether Viguerie and his New Right clients have the staying power for political survival. David Cohen of Common Cause questions whether the New Right groups represent "a citizens' movement or merely a direct mail movement." For the moment, however, the right wing is riding high, and the conservative political marketplace is a seller's dreamland.

But direct mail has inherent limitations. David Keane, a political consultant to Reagan and Gerald Ford, noted:

A direct mail message that is opened and read by the 2 percent true believers can be effective in a primary, but totally inappropriate when you need to get 51 percent in a general election. Then you must appeal to middle-of-the-road voters, and the hot, emotional rhetoric and issues which raise funds from the conservative faithful can be self-defeating.

The computerized slickness of direct mail can also go awry. In a 1976 Montana Senate race, Viguerie, in a stock "involvement device," had Republican Stanley Burger ask thousands of people to serve on his advisory committee. Burger was embarrassed when it turned out that he had invited his opponent, Senator John Melcher, as well as various members of Melcher's family and staff, to serve on the committee.

The continued effectiveness of lobbying Congress with mountains of prewritten cards and letters is also in doubt. Labor unions are retaliating with their own mass mail. "If Congress wants to respond to mail by tonnage," says the AFL-CIO's Ben Albert, "we'll equal their tonnage, hernias to postmen notwithstanding." An overwhelmed Congress is now installing its own answering machines—so that computers are talking to computers.

It is still not certain that a solid coalition can be shaped from voters who rise to the bait of a single, emotion-laden issue. For individual campaigns, maybe. But no one knows. The union member worked up against gun control and the Catholic housewife who believes that abortion is murder might not stick with conservatives on traditional bread-and-butter issues.

William Brock, chairman of the Republican National Committee, says Viguerie and the New Right are concentrating on the wrong issues:

You can't build a party around those emotional social issues, and I'm not sure government can solve them. The New Right groups are competitive not only in that they draw away money from us but they draw away attention in Congress from the broad issues of tax reduction, job creation, health care, housing—the American Dream issues. We can only become a majority party by bringing together people around those issues.

Unfortunately, for Democrats and Republicans alike, the vast majority of us are increasingly apathetic politically, and we permit the arena to be dominated by small, intensely partisan splinter groups. The answer, of course, is for more people to become more involved. The kind of citizen participation that is needed goes well beyond mailing a prewritten postcard to a member of Congress. But neither Richard Viguerie nor any other political wizard has a magic prescription to make a majority of Americans care about and participate in their government.

POLITICS AS A PERFORMING ART[2]

One Saturday a few years ago, those who like peeping at famous people would have gone crazy if they had strolled on the beach in front of the exclusive, mile-long Malibu Colony.

[2] Excerpted from "Hooray for Hollytics!?!" by Michele Willens, Los Angeles-based free-lance reporter. *Politics Today.* 6:36–40. Jl.–Ag. '79. © 1979 by Politics Today, Inc. All rights reserved. Reprinted by permission.

There on the patio of one of the million-dollar homes sat Paul Newman, Robert Redford, Warren Beatty and Neil Diamond sipping beers, munching on tortilla chips and engaging in a lengthy conversation with several other men. Even for Malibu, the scene was loaded with star power.

What sort of deal were the super four working up: perhaps *Butch & Sundance Get a Shampoo* with music by Neil Diamond? No, for that, their agents would probably have done the dickering. This was more personally important to the four. The men they were talking to were political activists, and the subject was divestiture, deregulation and other ways to tame the power of the major oil companies. What eventually resulted from that meeting was Energy Action, an anti-oil company lobby that today is considered the top national spokesman for the consumer side of energy issues.

The specifics of the oil debate aside, what is important to note is that the fuel for fighting the oil industry in this case came largely from the entertainment industry. Indeed there is scarcely a hot political issue today on which those in the politics business do not seek out those in show business. Not so much for the thoughts and insights of the stars. Not really to get them to speak out—though some like Anita Bryant and Jane Fonda can and do campaign effectively. The big reason is bucks. Successful show biz performers and executives not only earn big money themselves; they are expert in the business of drawing a paying crowd. More and more they are using that expertise to raise cash for political issues and candidates. "There isn't much difference between selling Donna Summer or Jerry Brown," says Richard Trugman matter of factly. He should know. He left a top job doing the former at Casablanca Records to do the latter as finance chairman of Brown's gubernatorial campaign last year. And he raised a hefty $4 million.

The only person who collected close to that in California that year was Republican Mike Curb, another former recording executive, who called on music friends and former clients like Wayne Newton, Steve Lawrence and Eydie

Gorme for fundraising help and successfully got himself elected lieutenant governor.

In the 1980 presidential campaign, the Washington-Hollywood connection will be more pronounced than ever. Pronounced enough so that it deserves a name of its own—one of those shiny, coined names that collapses words together. Hollytics will do fine. The big reason that Hollytics seems certain to grow in importance is that the campaign financing law now limits individual contributors to $1,000 and corporate giving to $5,000. But it does not limit contributions of time or talent. And when a Wayne Newton or a Paul Simon is willing to appear at a major concert for a candidate, tens and even hundreds of thousands of dollars can be raised from the ticket sales. That cash is then eligible for matching federal funds. In sum, Hollytics can add up.

Jimmy Carter found that out when his Georgia music executive friend, Phil Walden, got his clients, the Allman Brothers, to put on a concert in November 1975, that raised $100,000 (including the matching federal funds). "Carter had completely run out of money, but that concert saved him," contends Mickey Kantor, who ran Jerry Brown's brief 1976 presidential campaign—a campaign that itself was 40 percent funded by the entertainment industry. Ronald Reagan made only limited use of celebrities in 1976. Not so this time. "We've already got people like Frank Sinatra, Pat Boone, Jimmy Stewart and James Cagney committed," says Reagan campaign chief John Sears. Celebrities tend to lean left, but other frequent Republican supporters include Pearl Bailey, Chuck Connors and Shirley Temple Black.

The Reagan strategists are contemplating getting a full-time Hollytics specialist after the success of Trugman for Brown last year. Just as direct mail experts became the hottest new political operatives of the last decade, so experts at harnessing entertainers may become the mark of the eighties campaign. Already the presidential sweepstakes has started generating efforts to get star backing. Joe Smith, board chairman of Elektra/Asylum Records, reports that he has been bombarded with calls from candidates' camps hoping to line him up, along with his recording artists. . . .

Of course, the phenomenon of celebrities in politics goes far beyond the boundaries of Hollywood. Florida's Anita Bryant was able to take advantage of her fame in her anti-gay campaign. In New Jersey, Bill Bradley's winning Senate race was helped by the crowd-pulling glamour of basketball star Bradley himself, as well as celebrity friends such as Jack Nicholson, Chevy Chase and Dustin Hoffman. In Atlanta, entertainment lawyer David Franklin is yet another practitioner of the art. He mobilizes such clients as Gladys Knight, Roberta Flack, Cicely Tyson and Richard Pryor for candidates whom he supports. His backing was critical to the election of Atlanta Mayor Maynard Jackson, for example. Franklin, a middle-level member of the LBJ [Lyndon B. Johnson] administration, picks his candidates in part because of their positions and pledges on black issues.

But despite those examples, the center of the action is still Hollywood—where there is the heaviest concentration of those who can draw big crowds and those who know how to stage the big-draw events. Hollywood, in fact, has dabbled in politics on and off for years. In the early days of World War I, patriotism was an important political cause, and stars such as Mary Pickford, Douglas Fairbanks and Charlie Chaplin appeared in Los Angeles's Pershing Square to talk the crowd they attracted into buying Liberty Bonds. During World Ware II, Hollywood's patriotism reached even greater heights. Bob Hope, Martha Raye and others went overseas to entertain the troops and boost morale. Back home, Eddie Cantor headed up a marathon bond drive in 1944 that raised an astonishing $40 million in 24 hours.

Other more partisan political causes, such as the protecting of civil liberties, were aided by celebrity benefits, radio shows and movie premieres. And there were even those who rebelled against Hollywood's general spirit of superpatriotism and boosterism. Then came the Red-hunting hearings of the House Un-American Activities Committee in 1947. The infamous blacklist resulted, and all was quiet, politically, in Hol-

lywood for a long while after that. A few personalities, like
Bogart and Bacall, immersed themselves in Adlai Stevenson's
campaign, but there was little mingling of the two worlds.

The attitude began to shift again just before the start of
the sixties. "The combination of television and John Kennedy
brought out a lot of Hollywood people," says Jack Valenti,
the former LBJ aide who now heads the Motion Picture Association. "Politics was not really an intense emotion for many
until then. TV made politics more accessible, and in Kennedy, they saw someone as glamorous as anyone in America."
The glittering-glamour socializing slowly changed to political
commitment—as the Vietnam War slowly changed into a
cause célèbre. One of the first signs of the new attitude was
the Dissenting Democrats of 1968, spearheaded by actor Robert Vaughn; the group worked to open up the nomination
process to someone other than LBJ, then the sitting president.

For all that history, the ingredients that actually hold the
Washington-Hollywood connection together remain somewhat intangible. The two worlds have little in common other
than one's ability to raise money and the other's need to
spend it. Francis O'Brien, a former Mondale aide who is currently assistant to the president of Paramount Pictures, observes that "the attraction is they're both major power bases
filled with people in the business of exposing themselves.". . .

The first star to move beyond endorsement into the nitty-
gritty of campaign work, . . . [Warren Beatty] organized Hollywood behind a candidate better than anyone ever had when
he worked for George McGovern in 1972. The big names and
the bright stars brought McGovern far more media attention
than the conventional roster of political endorsements gained
for his Democratic rivals. It was also Beatty who first used the
political concert effectively, organizing three of them for
McGovern. "Warren was great because he knew just how to
handle the psychology of the stars," says businessman Miles
Rubin, who also worked on the concerts. "He was their intellectual guru, but he also surrounded them with enough glamour to make them feel at home." Beatty was relentless. Barbra
Streisand, one of the first stars to endorse McGovern,

made it clear that was all she would do. Months later, she had a phone call from Warren Beatty. Her first words to him were, "You want me to sing." He did, and she did.

Beatty has not been nearly so involved since. "You have to pull in and out of politics," he has said. Others have been more consistently concerned. Paul Newman falls into this group, though he tends to be more committed to issues than candidates. Newman prefers to stay out of the limelight but has probably contributed more money—over a million dollars—to political causes than anyone in Hollywood. He has given hundreds of thousands to the anti-oil company lobby group he helped create, Energy Action. When told about an idea for a nuclear war conference, Newman quietly wrote out a check for $50,000 to underwrite it. Sometimes uncomfortable about his inability to articulate issues, Newman nonetheless last year served as a delegate to the UN session on disarmament.

Robert Redford is also an issues man, though his focus is the single issue of ecology. He has been active in helping to stop power plants and has made appearances for a few candidates who support his views. Marlo Thomas is another single-issue political crusader; her cause is the women's movement. She contributes money and speaks all over the country on behalf of candidates. "I won't change votes, but people will listen to me," Thomas says. "I get a spotlight on me, then I turn it over to the candidate."

By any measure, Hollywood's queen in the political spotlight is Jane Fonda. To begin with, she is the only Hollywood figure with her own political organization. The Campaign for Economic Democracy (CED) is run by Tom Hayden, Fonda's husband, a former sixties radical and unsuccessful candidate for the US Senate in 1976. CED lobbies against big business and in favor of an assortment of Fonda-Hayden causes, including solar energy, rent control and farm workers. But Fonda does not support CED single-handedly. "The primary source of funding comes from concerts and the entertainment industry," says Hayden. "Entertainment people were and are helpful because they provide a fundraising base and ask very little in return." When they do ask for something, it is generally for professional rather than political favors. If you are wondering how Helen Reddy got Jane Fonda as her guest on a TV variety special, you should know that Reddy has given political contributions to Hayden.

Fonda's second front for pressing her political work is through her films. She has formed her own production company with partner Bruce Gilbert specifically to dramatize their political beliefs. . . . They have come up with two remarkable successes—*Coming Home* and *The China Syndrome.*

Fonda, who will probably work for Brown in the presidential campaign, is the most out-front mover and shaker. In contrast, Lew Wasserman, the enormously wealthy chairman of MCA (which owns Universal Studios), is the ultimate invisible power behind the scenes. For years he has been one of the industry's biggest political campaign contributors and a major fundraiser for the Democratic party. But his involvement is carefully even-handed. "There's no ideology with Lew," says one former associate. "He just has to be close to the center. He likes to be sure his bets are hedged and his company is on the good side of whoever is president."

He has been for the last 20 years. LBJ offered him the post of secretary of commerce. He has been mentioned publically as "my dear friend, Lew Wasserman," by Jimmy Carter. "I give them all money and wish them well," he explains. Of course, it is not quite so benign as all that. In 1964, for example, Wasserman let it be known that he wanted help on the advertising for LBJ's presidential campaign from an advertising firm that handled some work for Universal Studios. The firm's two partners, who opposed Johnson, refused despite the clear consequences. That was the end of their work for Universal.

Some believe, no doubt at their peril, that Wasserman, now in his mid-sixties, may have waning influence. They look to a somewhat newer breed of executive whose political interests have roots in feelings of social concern, rather than a desire to be close to the sources of power. Ted Ashley of

Warner Brothers is one such corporate chieftain. "One day I looked around and realized there was a whole world out there," Ashley says. In 1975 he quit his job, spent a year reading and thinking about political issues, then finally decided against playing a direct role in politics and returned to the studio. But he remains heavily involved and a few months ago was a key creator of Democrats for Change, a new group that took out a full-page ad in Los Angeles newspapers criticizing Carter.

Norman Lear, the other big power behind Democrats for Change, downplays the importance of personalities like himself. "I always think the strength is in numbers," he says. . . . If voters make a decision based on our names, they're misguided.

Of course, in a town where very large deals are made and unmade on a whim, it may not be misguided for a hopeful young producer to take a table at a testimonial dinner that is being put together by Wasserman. And if Robert Redford is hosting a party for Bill Bradley, as he did, many a high-income stargazer will pay $100 a couple for the privilege of saying who he had dinner with last night. And as for the concerts, fans who want to see Donny and Marie Osmond or the Eagles may not even care what candidate their ticket money is supporting.

The thousands who will pay to hear their favorite recording stars have made music executives perhaps the most important power elite of Hollytics. Get one of them, and his label's stable often follows. "I've been tyring to get artists to do at least one thing for someone else every year," Elektra/Asylum's Smith says. "They make an obscene amount of money, and I think they should have some kind of social responsibility." Neil Bogart, head of Casablanca Records and Filmworks, has also pushed his company's artists, including Kiss, Cher and Donna Summer, to think past their next gold disc for the first time.

Of all of the music moguls, none is more powerful—or at least none swings his power more—than Jeff Wald. With his wife, Helen Reddy, Wald has contributed over a million dollars, mainly to Democratic campaigns. Their big interest is Jerry Brown, and Wald may be getting ready to play a major role in Brown's presidential campaign. A tough-talking, hot-headed man of 36, Wald turns off a lot of people. "Jeff doesn't think," says another record executive. "He just wants to be buddies with a president." Wald is frank about why he likes the hard-ball game of politics. "Show business may give you ego gratification," he says, "but it's money that gives you real power. It's allowed me not to be helpless and to get things done. It allows me to use my leverage, and I quite definitely do it. I don't ask favors from anyone, but I have the power of money and access, and Helen has the power of visibility."

Some say Wald doesn't ask for favors, he demands them. One story has him twisting the arm of Los Angeles Mayor Tom Bradley about a decision that affected a nearby private school attended by Wald's children. Wald's tactic was to remind the mayor of past contributions. Bradley surprised many people when he decided in favor of Wald's position. Wald explained, "He did it on the advice of homeowner groups, not just mine."

Wald's relatively open power plays tend to undercut a prevailing bromide about Hollytics. That is that the money raised by performers comes with no strings attached. After all, says former Mondale aide O'Brien, "Jimmy Carter's not going to call Henry Winkler about SALT." And it is true that an oil company is likely to have a few more suggestions in mind than, say, Cher does.

But it is also true that many in show business are beginning to grasp and use the new clout they have. Wald, Fonda, Redford, Newman, the late John Wayne have all sought to affect policy—not insidiously, to be sure, but no less definitely than would mistrusted "fat cats" of the past. Sometimes the power wielded can balance out. Anita Bryant's drive to pass antigay legislation in Florida was matched by an equally successful campaign—led by many entertainment people—that defeated an antigay measure in California. But in other cases, there can be a considerable tilt. For example, entertainment people—and rock groups in particular—are overwhelmingly antinuclear.

Is all this show biz in the public business bad? Stars are not necessarily any dimmer than other politically influential business people. They may be no more disconnected from the common citizen than the intellectual power elite. But their growing importance certainly adds to the celebrification of politics. It is an era in which Elizabeth Taylor is an active member of the Senate Wives' Club. Linda Ronstadt may be the nation's next "first lady" (or perhaps the nation's first "main lady"). Sam Ervin leaves the Senate and makes American Express card commercials. Robert Byrd records an album of bluegrass fiddle music. Henry Kissinger becomes a paid TV commentator while Jerry Ford does the same and gets canceled. John Lindsay plays a senator in a movie and now considers running to become a real one. The distinctions between leadership and glamour continue to blur. Henry Fonda, Jason Robards and Rip Torn all seem to have had higher approval ratings for their performances as presidents than have any recent incumbents.

But hold on. *The China Syndrome* was not the Three Mile Island accident. John Dean was not just a TV series. The Vietnam War has reality beyond that shown in *The Deerhunter. The Omen* is not a real story about how the devil is on his way to taking over the US. The phantasmagoric overlap of Washington and Hollywood can be sorted out.

Still it does exist. Last year a politically bland candidate named Carey Peck ran for Congress in Los Angeles. He was running against Robert Dornan, an incumbent Republican who was thought to be unbeatable. Carey Peck, however, is the son of Gregory Peck, and the actor summoned a host of his Democratic friends, including Liza Minnelli, Milton Berle and Kirk Douglas, who performed at campaign dinners. Dornan countered with John Wayne, Gene Autry and Pat Boone—and narrowly won.

If that race is a harbinger of more and more campaigns, then Hollytics is already overweening. Such a stars war is a spectacle of the sorrier sort—but for now spectacle and show

biz involvement in US politics seem likely to grow larger.
Spotlights still draw too many of us.

REFERENDUM FEVER[3]

In this era of alienation, one flickering life sign still ani-
mates the body politic. Public confidence in all branches and
levels of government is eroding. For the first time, a plurality
of the electorate refuses to identify itself with either party.
Election turnout has dwindled to such an extent that a quarter of the eligible voters may choose the next President, and
of those who did bother to vote in 1978, fully 40 percent, according to an NBC/Associated Press survey, believed it made
no real difference who was elected. Yet, in the face of this apathy and cynicism, the referendum is booming.

In the 1978 elections, California's Proposition 13 received
more media attention and had greater national impact than
any senatorial or gubernatorial race, perhaps more than any
nonpresidential contest since Lincoln confronted Douglas in
1858. American voters decided more than 350 other statewide referenda—a record for off-year elections—and thousands of local questions. Some of these were measures routinely submitted to the electorate after legislative approval,
but many came from the grass roots through the initiative
process.

Proponents of "direct democracy" are pushing hard in
every arena to extend its use. California Governor Jerry
Brown, leading the crusade for a balanced budget amendment, is trying an end run on the Washington political establishment by calling for the first constitutional convention
since 1787. In Texas and New York, the only large states
without referenda, movements are afoot to implement them.

[3] Reprint of magazine article by André Mayer, historian, and Michael Wheeler,
professor, New England School of Law. *Atlantic.* 244:53-5. S. '79. Copyright © 1979, by
The Atlantic Monthly Company, Boston, Mass. Reprinted with permission.

Minnesota's new governor, Albert Quie, wants to require voter approval for any new taxes. A federal referendum is the goal of Initiative America, a Washington-based group dominated by left-liberal veterans of the antiwar movement; it is also favored three to one by readers of *Nation's Business*. Advocates wave friendly polls: Pat Caddell reports that 74 percent of Americans would be "more inclined to go to vote if they could vote on issues as well as candidates."

Like its religious counterpart, this political revivalism offers the promise of renewal for a tired faith, but the proselytizing zeal of its converts tends to polarize more than persuade. The obvious appeal of direct democracy, the people's recourse against corruption, special interests, and bureaucracy, is set against the claims of republican pluralism. On the level of expediency, liberal and conservative camps alike are divided between optimists who are sure the *vox populi* will speak their language and pessimists who live in fear of the unrestrained Yahoos.

Amid the polemics, we have heard little reasoned analysis of the referendum as an integral element of our constitutional structure. Direct democracy, after all, has a long history in our political life, with roots going back to the New England town meeting. The earliest statewide referendum took place in 1778, when Massachusetts voters rejected a proposed constitution. Two years later they approved the present version, and the right of Americans to participate directly in formulating their fundamental laws was established. The referendum also has a recognized function as a device to keep politicians responsive to the public will by allowing citizens an alternative means of expression. In Woodrow Wilson's phrase, it is "the gun behind the door." Thus its popularity in these cynical and apathetic times is no paradox—these are the precise circumstances under which Americans have a need for its distinctive constitutional role.

Because of its sporadic remedial use, and because it does not exist at the national level, we have never fully assimilated direct democracy into our political consciousness. Though as ancient as the other components of our polity, it has not

passed through the same process of evolution and refinement.
Even the electoral reforms of the past decade, themselves a
product of the conditions that revived direct democracy,
have left referendum procedures virtually untouched.

For a telling illustration of some of the unresolved problems, we need look no further than the 1978 Massachusetts
ballot, the bicentennial edition, as it were, of America's first
venture into large-scale direct democracy. As in most states,
voters had to wade through a clutter of trivia to find the important questions. In addition to purely local issues, and non-
binding instructions to legislators on subjects ranging from tax
reform and nuclear power to sanitary landfill, four inconse-
quential matters of governmental housekeeping appeared in
the impressive guise of amendments to the state constitution.
Revisions of census and informational mailing procedures
passed easily; 73 percent of the voters approved granting in-
coming governors more time to submit a budget, but only 52
percent were similarly lenient with city charter commissions.
When the issues are technical and interest is low, the public
can be cranky.

The most hotly debated question on the ballot was a property tax classification amendment, authorizing higher rates
for businesses than for residences. Boston Mayor Kevin White
commandeered more than a million dollars in city funds to
stump for the measure, while a well-financed opposition
warned that the plan would drive away industry, throw people out of work, fuel inflation, and actually increase taxes for
homeowners.

Although more money was spent on this question than on
any race for elective office, little light was shed on the real
issues. Indeed, the basic tactic of the opponents seemed to be
to scare voters by confusing them about the proposition's implications; however, proponents managed to make the consequences of non-passage seem equally unpredictable, and the
amendment was approved. Courts subsequently rejected
White's use of public funds in the campaign, but upheld the
result of the vote. The Mayor's exploitation of the referendum
to enhance his own image and build his organization may sig-

nal a new kind of political coattailing which evades campaign finance laws. Howard Jarvis may have been the wrong man in the right place.

A separate statewide question raised similar issues, but somehow escaped public debate. Massachusetts voters were asked to consider a proposed constitutional amendment which, according to the ballot summary, would permit lower property taxes "for land which is used for recreation purposes and for land preserved in its natural state." The summary reminded voters that owners of "wild and forest land" already enjoyed tax relief, and added that the new provision's purpose was "to develop and conserve natural resources and the environmental benefits of recreational land."

By better than three to two, citizens cast their ballots for rolling hills, sparkling water, and white sand. Few realized that the law had been conceived and promoted by the Massachusetts Golf Association as a special tax break for country clubs and private golf course owners. Club members can now enjoy lower dues while everyone else in town, even those who have been blackballed by the admissions committee, must pick up the slack. Perhaps golf courses are community assets, but any tax subsidy for private interests should be proposed forthrightly. That supporters of the amendment felt compelled to mask its true purpose suggests that they knew it could not survive open debate.

A related referendum tactic is to seek support for self-serving measures by sweetening them with promised public benefits. In 1976 proponents of greyhound racing in California tried to seduce various voting blocs by phrasing the proposition to suggest that added state revenues would be dispersed to high school athletics and aid to the blind, senior citizens, and working mothers.

The most pernicious proposition on the Massachusetts ballot was one which, like the pro-golf amendment, has appeared in several other states. It offered a constitutional amendment which, according to the summary, "would provide that a student could neither be assigned nor denied admittance to a public school on the basis of race, color,

national origin or creed." The language deliberately mim-
icked antidiscrimination laws, but its actual purpose was to
ban busing for school desegregation. This ambiguity may
have cut both ways, but in any case, the amendment passed
overwhelmingly. The deceptive wording aside, the proposition patently violates civil rights guarantees of the federal
constitution, and thus cannot be of any legal force.

The increasing popularity of direct democracy, particularly in matters of broad social policy, has resulted in a growing number of such unconstitutional referendum questions.
Most of the controversial initiatives approved by California
voters in recent years have been invalidated, wholly or in
part, by the courts. Some commentators have argued that a
protest vote is justifiable as an outlet for political anger or as a
way to "send a message" to Washington or the State House,
but neither of these is an appropriate function for the referendum. If the voters unwittingly adopt a measure later declared
unconstitutional, frustration and alienation will be heightened. If voters do so deliberately, the exercise can hardly be
deemed the considered act of responsible citizens.

Use of the referendum for purposes best left to public
opinion polls and letters to elected representatives can only
devalue the process of direct democracy and justify the fears
of those who claim that the American voter does not take his
or her politics seriously enough to be trusted with unlimited
power.

In a political world seemingly seized with inertia, it is se-
ductive to think we can solve our most pressing social and
economic problems with a simple yes or no vote. When voters
feel more and more distant from their representatives, it is
not surprising that people want to take power into their own
hands. Unfortunately, the most obvious recourse, the referendum, is a very crude implement for policy-making in a complex society.

At a town meeting, with all the voters face-to-face in a
single room, proposals can be explained, debated, revised,
even tabled pending further discussion. Here, direct democ-

racy works. On the state level, let alone on a national scale, we cannot hope to reproduce this same flexibility. There are, however, certain steps we should take to ensure that the results of future referenda represent as clear an expression of carefully considered voter opinion as possible.

First, we must clean up our ballots. As referendum questions proliferate, voter confusion increases, and matters of the greatest long-term importance may be lost among the trivia or overshadowed by momentarily more controversial issues. When one of the ballot questions is whether dental technicians should be allowed to fit false teeth (as was the case in Oregon), citizens may be tempted to write off the whole process as either silly or technical.

To reduce the number of propositions by increasing the number of petitioners required to place questions on the ballot would simply reinforce the power of the richest and best organized interest groups; stricter requirements would not stop the flow of questions sent to the voters by the legislatures. Since many of these are amendments to our over-detailed state constitutions, they cannot be removed from the ballot entirely. Perhaps, however, questions could be segregated according to the degree of controversy attached to them. Statewide initiatives and referenda approved by relatively close legislative votes might be placed on the general election ballots, while routine matters could be presented in the primaries.

This raises a second point—the timing of referenda. Nothing could be worse than the widespread practice of deciding controversial ballot questions in state primaries when the voters are few and are often skewed by unequal interest in party contests. Moreover, high participation by supporters of a single referendum question might easily affect candidate selection. Special referendum elections can allow fuller consideration of the issues, but may be exploited by well-organized interest groups if turnout is low. No solution is perfect, but it is clear that the general election ballot is the place for important referendum questions.

Third, we must clarify the meaning of referendum questions. Some recent consumer legislation requires insurance companies to write their policies in "plain English." It is absurd that we do not require at least as much for ballot questions. Bipartisan commissions should certify questions and oversee voter information programs. We castigate George Gallup and his ilk whenever they ask slanted questions, but at least their polls do not become law. Allowing private country clubs to masquerade as environmentalists is little different from letting candidates run under assumed names.

Fourth, referendum questions should be screened for constitutionality before they are placed on the ballot. In some states, courts can render advisory opinions on pending legislation; the same mechanism could be used for plebiscites. Although an ultimate ruling on a proposal's validity might have to wait for an actual case, a preliminary reading could guide voters and sharpen debate.

Finally, while simplifying the questions, we should consider allowing more precise answers. At present, voters who are undecided about a proposal, or who favor it only with modifications, are trapped by the yes-or-no format of the ballot. If they refrain from voting, their opinions, however strong, count for nothing; if they vote no, they express a commitment they do not feel. A third, "none of the above" option, or the requirement that a proposition receive a majority of all ballots cast, including blanks, would allow voters to call for further alternatives while freeing legislatures from the incubus of an ill-considered or unintended public "mandate."

Reform is all the more urgent because First Amendment safeguards may well preclude regulation of referendum campaign finance. Last year, the Supreme Court struck down a prohibition against corporate spending to influence such elections. Fortunately, the danger of corruption here is not bribery, but voter ignorance and the use of modern publicity techniques to confuse instead of enlighten.

DIRECT DEMOCRACY: THE INITIATIVE[4]

Americans in the Seventies did not turn away from the politics of direct action, they merely domesticated it, institutionalized it, and embraced it in the bosom of the middle class.

Nothing illustrates this better than the rising use of the initiative, a device by which—in the 23 states and more than 100 cities that allow it—citizens can draft a piece of legislation, place it on the ballot by petition, and have their fellow voters directly decide on election day whether it should become law or not. (Initiatives are different from referendums, which allow voters to accept or reject laws already passed by the legislature.) By the end of 1979, some 175 initiatives will have been voted on at the state level since 1970, almost twice as many as in the 1960s. The rate of initiative use accelerated through the decade, from 10 in 1970 to more than 40 each in 1976 and 1978. Two states and the District of Columbia have added the initiative process to their constitutions, and at least 10 others now are considering doing so. In one of them, New York, the initiative idea is being pushed by an unlikely coalition of the League of Women Voters, the Conservative Party, the local branch of Ralph Nader's Public Interest Research Group, and an ad hoc organization called V.O.T.E., which is headed by a conservative investment banker who says he hopes to become New York's Howard Jarvis.

Coalitions like this one (which, to confuse matters further, bears the editorial imprimatur of the *New York Times* and *Newsday*, as well as a host of conservative upstate newspapers) make it hard to characterize the rising initiative tide in standard liberal-conservative terms. So does the sponsorship in Congress of the proposed constitutional amendment to

[4] Excerpted from magazine article "Power to the People: The Crusade for Direct Democracy," by Michael Nelson, political science faculty, Vanderbilt University, and contributing editor of *Washington Monthly. Saturday Review.* 6:12-14+. N. 24, '79. © 1979 by Saturday Review Magazine Corp. All rights reserved. Reprinted by permission.

allow national initiatives, which ranges from senators like
Mark Hatfield on the left to Dennis DeConcini in the middle
and Larry Pressler on the right. Among conservative columnists, George F. Will has condemned the initiative, Patrick
Buchanan has praised it, and James J. Kilpatrick has been all
over the lot. Liberals such as Tom Wicker (pro) and the *New
Republic*'s Henry Fairlie (con) can be found on either side.

Most distressing of all to those who like their politics tidy
has been the extraordinary range of purposes to which the initiative has been put. Last year, for example, Oregon voters
passed an initiative that restored capital punishment, but defeated one to restrict state funding of abortions. (They also
decided to break the dentists' monopoly on the sale of false
teeth.) Michigan voted to raise the drinking age from 19 to
21, but spurned a conservative educational "voucher" plan
that would have subsidized parents' decisions to send their
children to private schools. (Californians may be voting on a
similar plan next June.) An Alaska initiative to set aside some
30 million acres of land for small homesteaders was approved;
another to ban no-deposit bottles failed. Californians turned
down an anti-smoking proposal; they also refused to require
school boards to fire homosexual teachers. A Montana initiative to place restrictions on nuclear power-plant licensing
and operations won. A North Dakota plan to regulate health-
care costs lost. Collective-bargaining rights did well in Michigan and Missouri, while casino gambling did poorly in
Florida.

The most celebrated initiative of 1978 was, of course, California's Proposition 13, the astonishingly popular proposal by
Howard Jarvis and Paul Gann to reduce property taxes in the
state by 57 percent. Its success in June quickly triggered a
middle-class "tax revolt" that terrified liberals in other states.
James Farmer, the erstwhile civil rights leader who now
heads a group called the Coalition of American Public Employees, complained that "the tax revolt represents nothing
more than the overthrow of equity among taxpayers." Worried commentators predicted that right-wing Jarvis fever
would sweep the initiative states in November.

It did not quite turn out that way, however. Although Proposition 13 clones passed in two small states, Idaho and Nevada, they failed in Michigan and Oregon. Four state initiatives to limit increases in government spending passed, but two were turned down. Still others failed to garner enough signatures to get on the ballot. This year Nevada voters repealed the state's 3.5 percent sales tax on food, a reform dear to liberal hearts. And next year a whole host of tax initiatives—liberal, conservative, or both—will come up at the polls. Ohio and Massachusetts proposals (as described in "Renegade Tax Reform: Turning Prop 13 on Its Head" [see excerpt in Section III]) would cut property taxes but make up the lost revenues with increased levies on business. Interestingly enough, political scientist Austin Ranney found that in the 33 years prior to 1978, the initiative served as a tool for liberals on tax issues. Their side triumphed 77 percent of the time.

The lack of a clear ideological tilt in the initiative process also is evidenced by the new style of initiative politicians who have led the direct-action efforts of the 1970s. Thus far, arch-conservative Howard Jarvis is the one national celebrity to come out of the initiative movement—he even made *People* magazine's list of "The 25 Most Intriguing People of 1978." But Pat Quinn of Chicago is a more typical wielder of the initiative tool. Quinn is a full-time law student at Northwestern University who, as "a 40-hour-a-week hobby," heads an 8,000 member organization called the Illinois Coalition for Political Honesty. . . .

Quinn, a young liberal, and Jarvis, an aging conservative, have a good bit more in common than first meets the eye. So do the conservative tax "revolters" in Idaho and the liberal tax "reformers" in Ohio, the conservative pro-voucher people in California and the liberal anti-dentists in Oregon, and other seemingly dissimilar groups of activists. For whatever their political coloration, the greater part of initiative users seem motivated by a basic shared concern: They regard the government itself as just another self-serving interest, one that is all the more threatening because it cannot be reformed except from outside, through direct-action politics.

Looking back over the history of political reform in this century, it is remarkable how many fundamental political changes were hastened by initiative after state legislators balked, reluctant to alter the rules of the game by which they had been elected. Long before Congress and the state legislatures saw the handwriting on the wall, initiatives in several states already had been passed to repeal the poll tax, establish woman suffrage, provide for direct election of United States senators, and institute primary elections. Similarly, the Seventies have been marked by a whole host of ethics, disclosure, and "sunshine-in-government" initiatives, passed by voters after legislatures had turned them down. Austin Ranney finds that historically, the initiative has been used more to alter governmental and political processes than for any other purpose.

In this light, it also seems apparent that the Proposition 13-inspired "tax revolt" has been aimed less at taxes per se than at the ever larger and more prosperous government bureaucracies that are collecting and spending them. In California, for example, powerful government-employee unions, along with their colleagues in the legislature, beat back fairly modest efforts to reduce evermore burdensome property taxes for years, even after the state treasury accumulated a multibillion-dollar surplus. Finally, things reached the point where the lamentations of public officials simply were not believed. One poll taken on the eve of Proposition 13 found 88 percent of Californians insisting that "if government services were made more efficient, the current level of services could be provided even though budgets were reduced."

This perception of selfish behavior *by* government officials *for* government officials seems to exist among voters everywhere. A nationwide survey commissioned by the *Washington Post* found that three out of four citizens said they too would vote for a Proposition 13-style tax cut if they had the chance. But an even higher percentage also said that it wasn't so much the taxes that bothered them as the way the money was being wasted. Given a choice of low taxes or high taxes that are spent efficiently, two-thirds picked the latter. "Their real concern," the *Post* concluded, "is that it is the bureaucracy, not the public, that benefits from taxes." . . .

It was inevitable . . . that someone would take the initiative to Washington.

As it turned out, there were two people. John Forster and Roger Telschow, fresh out of college, had spent 1976 working in state initiative campaigns all over the country. "We were really struck at the time by the contrast between the enthusiasm people had about initiatives and the indifference they felt toward the presidential and congressional elections," says Telschow. After the election, the figures bore them out: Though voter turnout had dropped for the fourth straight time since 1960, initiative use reached a postwar high. Deciding that national initiatives on citizen-proposed federal laws were an idea whose time had come, they set off for Washington to try to get Congress to pass a constitutional amendment permitting such an innovation. Here is how the national initiative would work:

Citizens initiating a new law would have 18 months to collect petitions with valid signatures equal in number to 3 percent of the votes cast in the preceding presidential election—at present that would be 2.5 million. The Justice Department would then check the signatures for validity. If it certified them within 120 days of the next national election, the proposed initiative would go on the ballot right away; otherwise it would have to wait two years until the next election.

The initiative, if passed by a simple majority of voters, would become law 30 days after the election. As with any other legislation, it would be subject to judicial review and congressional override, though the latter would require the two-thirds vote of Congress and presidential concurrence. Finally, the initiative could not be used to declare war, call up troops, or propose constitutional amendments.

Initiative America (which is what the two young men named their organization) can be described generously as a shoestring operation. . . . But through sheer energy, will, and talent, Forster and Telschow managed to do everything a shoestring operation can do in politics. In 1977, they persuaded Senator James Abourezk to sponsor their amendment. They then roused interest among press and pollsters—Cambridge Survey Research found three-to-one public support for the idea, for example, and George Gallup included it in a *Reader's Digest* article on the "Six Political Reforms Americans Want Most." Because of this attention, and because Abourezk was a member of the constitutional amendments subcommittee, Senate hearings soon were held on it. . . . Forster and Telschow felt that once Senate hearings rendered the idea respectable, they would be able to rally a coalition of open-government groups like Common Cause behind it.

What followed was a bitterly disappointing experience, one that illustrates yet another sociological axiom: Adversarial organizations end up more alike than different.

We found out that these Washington-based "people's groups" have become little bureaucracies of their own [recalls Forster]. They see the initiative as a threat to their interests. They thrive on the fact that they can claim to represent people to the government on various issues. If people had an initiative to turn to, two things would happen: One, they could represent themselves, and two, the scene of the action would shift from Washington to the country. That would diminish the public-interest groups' importance. They prefer not to change the rules, even if there doesn't seem to be any chance of winning under the status quo.

Stalled in the Washington community, Initiative America's great hope for the future is that its proposal will be picked up in next year's presidential campaign. This would not be altogether surprising. The governing class's popular standing has been steadily declining. Support for the initiative amendment may prove a constructive way of tapping the public's dissatisfaction. So far, only Jimmy Carter and Howard Baker have brushed off Initiative America, and Jerry Brown, Ronald Reagan, Edward Kennedy, and John Connally are among those who at least have expressed interest. . . .

Although it is far from certain that the 1980s will see the

adoption of the national initiative amendment, there are a couple of predictions about the coming decade we can safely make.

The first is that, with the bicentennial of the Constitution looming in 1987, we are going to be hearing more than ever about the "intentions of the framers." In the case of the national initiative amendment, those intentions should be fairly easy to ascertain. Democracy was a dirty word at the Philadelphia convention—speakers used it only to raise the specter of mob rule and demagoguery—and any proposal to allow citizens to initiate and decide laws on their own surely would have been hooted off the floor.

Should we be bound by this? No, and I don't think the Founding Fathers (Warren Harding's phrase, not theirs) would want us to be so bound, any more than they would have when we abolished the poll tax, required direct election of senators, and gave the vote to blacks and women—other proposals that were or would have been dismissed at the Constitutional Convention. The authors of the Constitution were aware that they had no monopoly on truth for the ages. Indeed, their most important intention was that the plan of government they drafted by able to adapt to changing times and new kinds of experience. That is why they defined the nature and powers of its institutions in flexible language and why they included an amendment process.

Changing conditions have already altered the nature of our political system, in ways that make the initiative now seem constitutionally appropriate.

Admittedly [argues Professor Henry Abraham of the University of Virginia] the Founding Fathers envisaged lawmaking to be the province of the people's representatives in assembled Congress, but as our history has demonstrated, laws—or, if one prefers, policies *cum* laws—are increasingly made and applied not only by Congress but by the Chief Executive; by the host of all-but-uncontrollable civil servants in the executive agencies and bureaus; and by the judiciary. Why not permit another element of our societal structure to enter the legislative realm, namely, the people in their sovereign capacity as the ultimate repositor of power under our system, as envisaged by the letter and the spirit of the Preamble to the Constitution?

As Abraham suggests, the theories of the framers about how their plan of government really would work out in practice were just that—theories. Seventy-five years of experience with state initiatives (Oregon held the first one in 1904) can be safely said to have demonstrated the groundlessness of their fears. Historically, only about one-fifth of the initiatives filed have gotten enough petition signatures even to reach the ballot. And only about one-third of those that have reached the ballot have been passed by voters. This is hardly the "mobocracy" the framers feared democracy would breed.

The other sure prediction that we can make about the 1980s is that the politics of direct action will become even more widespread. For not only has initiative use been increasing, but also the use of other pressure tactics that lie outside the normal processes of representative democracy— with no sign that the basic dissatisfactions with the governing class that have caused all this are abating. Demonstrations, for example, now seem as American as apple pie. In Washington alone, the National Park Service currently issues a record 750 to 1,000 demonstration permits every year, many of them to groups opposing abortion, Equal Rights Amendment proponents, tractor-driving farmers, and other activists from the middle class. Surveying a wide range of poll data, political scientists Robert Gilmour and Robert Lamb recently concluded that "Mass protest, civil disobedience, and illegal disruption are now a part of the accepted political scene."

The Seventies also saw the rise of forms of direct-action politics that Sixties activists overlooked. The most spectacular recent example is the movement for a constitutional convention to consider a balanced-budget amendment. Presently, 30 states have demanded that Congress issue such a call, only four short of the required two-thirds. . . .

There is no telling what innovations the Eighties will bring in the way of direct-action politics—in Columbus, Ohio, people are already "participating" in televised local government meetings through their two-way cable television system. But whatever these innovations may be, they probably will make the initiative look good to its current opponents by comparison. The initiative is, after all, a technique of the ballot, not the streets or the living room. This not only makes it close kin to the standard system of representative democracy, but it also seems to strengthen that system in the long run. Thus political scientist Charles Bell recently reported that "half the high [election] turnout states use the initiative while only 14 percent of the low-turnout states use it." A Caddell poll found that 74 percent of the voters said they would be more inclined to vote in candidate elections if they also could vote on issues. And far from weakening state legislatures, initiatives seem to prod them on to better things. Eight of the 10 legislatures ranked highest by the Citizens Conference on State Legislatures are in initiative states.

The assault on the governing class of officials will continue. Whether it will come through the ballot box or some less pleasant route is up to them.

REWRITING THE CONSTITUTION[5]

Who do you like for president of the next constitutional convention—Sam Ervin or Archibald Cox? Take your time deciding, but do not take too long; the drive for a convention to require a balanced budget is bearing in on Washington. Officials there are hurrying to avoid it, but the thirty-fourth state could call for a convention within months. Then Congress would have to decide what to do about it, and the stakes could not be higher.

The call for a balanced budget has been raised to draw official Washington's attention finally to taxes, inflation, and a rising sense that government is out of control. It is a summary

[5] Excerpted from magazine article by Ben Martin, who teaches politics at the University of Missouri at Kansas City. *Harper's.* 259:26–28+. S. '79. Copyright © 1979 by Harper's Magazine. All rights reserved. Reprinted from the September issue by special permission.

complaint against the growth of government, reflecting a
basic insight that getting and spending, along with regulation,
are the heart of public policy. It steps over piecemeal issues,
and the demand for constitutional amendment underscores
the seriousness of the complaint. (*Article V.* "The Congress,
whenever two thirds of both houses shall deem it necessary,
shall propose Amendments to this Constitution, or, on the
Application of the Legislatures of two thirds of the several
States, shall call a Convention for proposing Amendments,
which, in either Case, shall be valid to all Intents and Purposes, as Part of this Constitution, when ratified by the Legislatures of three fourths of the several States, or by
Conventions in three fourths thereof, as the one or the other
Mode of Ratification may be proposed by the Congress.")

The states have petitioned for a balanced budget, but limiting government spending is more nearly the matter. "Balanced budget" is a slogan that makes sense in individuals'
terms, but on the federal level even higher taxes to balance
government spending is the last thing advocates want. Another scheme—perhaps more sensible—would tie annual
spending to increases in the gross national product.

Both ideas are enormously popular. In July, 1978, a Gallup survey found 81 percent polled favoring an amendment
requiring a balanced budget, though the figure slipped to 70
percent in an AP/NBC poll last February. And a CBS
News/*New York Times* poll last November found 76 percent
favoring a cut in spending over a tax cut. Yet people are real-
istic: 70 percent doubted politicians will work to balance the
budget.

Americans still display overwhelming support for the
Constitution. At the same time, there is widespread disaffection and a sense of distance from government. The Harris poll
found alienation from politics has doubled in a decade. Most
believe the American condition is worse now than in the past,
and they also feel things will not improve. For the first time,
there is personal pessimism as well; a majority now feel that
their personal situations will deteriorate in the future, along
with the country as a whole. And they pin the blame on

Washington. Fewer have confidence in the central government than in state and local governments, and confidence levels are lower overall for governmental than for private institutions—except for organized labor, which is distrusted as much as the federal government.

The states have applied to Congress hundreds of times before, for a wide range of amendments, but this time Washington is worried. With the steady centralization of power and the emergence of a national press, the vectors of cultural and political innovation seemed clear: elite to mass, Washington to hinterland, figurative center to periphery. But now, out of nowhere—out of state legislatures, of all places—comes this vulgar threat to the American mandarinate.

What passes for leadership of the movement comes from something called the National Taxpayers Union, although a Maryland state senator, James Clark, has also been pushing the idea with other state legislators since 1974. Since the Supreme Court has held that no individual taxpayer has standing to sue Congress over spending from the general treasury, the drive to limit spending constitutionally amounts to a grand, political class-action suit by taxpayers. The convention mode is the closest thing there is in the Constitution to the techniques of popular initiative and referendum, reflecting popular distrust of political establishments.

State legislators calling for a balanced budget are seen in Washington as traitors to the official class, siding with the voters against their big brothers at the national level and making them look bad. Accordingly, the first response in the capital was to threaten to shut off the federal money spigot to the states and localities: you want less spending, goodbye revenue sharing. This has had a sobering effect; state governors are already complaining about punitive blackmail from Washington.

Liberal Democrats generally oppose, in increasing order of ferocity: requiring a balanced budget; doing it by constitutional amendment; and doing that in another constitutional convention. Republicans in Washington also oppose a convention, but favor a balanced budget and are moving toward the method of amendment. The House Republican Policy Committee endorsed both a constitutionally required balanced budget and a limit on federal spending last spring, but party leaders in both chambers oppose another convention.

Jerry Brown of California is trying to ride the west wind by supporting all three, while Jimmy Carter of Washington opposes them. Brown's embrace of Proposition 13 last year assured his reelection as governor, but his support for a constitutional convention has hurt his chances for the Presidential nomination, at least in the party of government subsidy. He has little support among union leaders, Democratic regulars, and political activists who are more liberal than the rank-and-file but who dominate the party's organization. They have little love for Carter and may pine for Kennedy, but Brown's endorsement of a balanced-budget amendment is considered heresy and may have disqualified him even as stalking horse for Kennedy. . . .

Spending is politically profitable; taxing is not. Inflation conveniently pushes taxpayers into higher brackets, even when purchasing power declines, and tax revenues increase automatically. Spending can then rise, illusory "tax cuts" can be made noisily every few years, and government can grow.

In the past twenty-five years, the proportion of the income of the average American family taken in taxes has doubled. Federal, state, and local taxes now take more than a third of the net national product. Where does it all go? Neo-Keynesian theory helps justify government spending to stimulate demand, but it says nothing about who the payers and payees ought to be. Liberal Democratic social theory and constituency interests provide the answer: they should be different people. In the 1970s, for the first time in our history, the primary business of the central government became the transfer of income among individuals. Those in the upper half of adjusted gross incomes (above $8,931 in 1975) paid ninety-three percent of all the personal income taxes collected by the Internal Revenue Service, while purposeful transfer programs accounted for more than half of all the spending. This has created a growing class of permanent government dependents who see their subsidies as entitlements and who, together with public bureaucrats, provide vital support for the Democratic party.

The calls for a constitutional amendment to require a balanced budget are an attempt to check the growth of the share of the national income taken by government. Some think an amendment that limits spending would accomplish that more directly, since taxes could be raised to balance any budget. The National Tax Limitation Committee, led by [conservative economist] Milton Friedman, has proposed an amendment to Congress that would limit federal spending hikes to increases in the GNP, with a downward adjustment for inflation that would give politicians an incentive for reducing inflation rather than increasing it, as at present.

In practice, both ideas, balancing budgets and limiting spending, might tend to have the same effects. Taxpayers' complaints would slow the rise in taxes—and therefore spending—a bit if balanced budgets were required; and inflation-swollen taxes would quickly rise enough to balance the budget if spending were limited by law. Both amendments contain escape clauses that would free spending in case of national emergency, but neo-Keynesian economists—and President Carter—still claim they are insufficiently flexible to fight recessions.

Of course, inflexibility is the whole point of these spending limitations. Like locked liquor cabinets, they are intended to prevent larceny and intemperance in those we mistrust. Washington is a conglomerate of subgovernments—coteries of Congressmen and their staffs, bureaucrats, and lobbyists— concerned with different policy areas. Each of these iron triangles serves itself and its constituents in the short term, and the logrolling among them produces total spending and policy outcomes of unexpected proportions. The sluice points monitored by party leadership, the Congressional Budget Committees, and the Office of Management and Budget are unable to check the great flow of policy and spending. The proposed amendments to control the budget, are appropriately, determinedly *constitutional,* to govern profligate im-

pulses when self-discipline is absent and resolution inadequate.

Democrats in Congress want to give resolution another
try. The defeat of many liberal Democrats . . . [in 1978] and
the threat of the constitutional convention have been instruc-
tive. Suddenly, many are for a balanced budget—but not by
constitutional amendment. And few are willing to risk another convention. Democrats have lost five of the six special
elections for House seats since Carter's election; however,
most members can rely on their anonymity and the advantages of office they have bought themselves to assure reelection.

The most worried are those deficit spenders in the Senate
who feasted on the spoils of Watergate in 1974, but who now
must face a less distracted electorate: Gary Hart of Colorado,
Patrick Leahy of Vermont, John Durkin of New Hampshire,
John Culver, George McGovern, Frank Church, Birch Bayh.
They are getting their campaigns started earlier than usual,
putting distance between themselves and Carter, and hoping
the voters overlook the unbalanced budget in favor of all the
water projects they've lugged into their states.

But fiscal 1981 is the year the Congressional Budget Committees are planning a balanced budget, for the first time in
more than a decade, though only after another $23-billion
deficit in fiscal 1980, the fruit of Carter's "austerity." They
may make it, too, because inflation is pushing tax receipts so
high so fast that the 1981 budget could be balanced with even
enough left over for a tax cut of some $15 billion.

That would meet Carter's campaign promise of 1976, but
Congressional leaders are also hoping the promise of a balanced budget in just a couple of years will reduce pressure on
state legislatures for another constitutional convention. In
1980, it would remain only that—a promise—but that is
probably the best the Democrats can do.

President Carter has called the proposal for a second convention "extremely dangerous," citing fears that it might
throw out the Bill of Rights and undermine civil liberties, a
curious reaction from a candidate who only wanted to make

the government as good as the American people. But opponents believe that the American people would not be represented at another convention; it would be dominated by special interests.

If another convention were called, Congress would try to restrict its deliberations to the budget amendment, although most legal scholars doubt the validity of such an attempt. Prof. Charles Black of Yale Law School feels the framers intended the Congressional method for piecemeal amendment and the convention mode only when so many were dissatisfied with their government that a general revision was necessary. All the state applications for a balanced-budget amendment have limited their call specifically to that subject, and some have called for a convention only if Congress fails to initiate such an amendment; but, once gathered, the delegates could argue convincingly that they were entitled to set their own agenda, and such a runaway assembly is the stunning possibility that mesmerizes everyone. At the furthest edge of plausibility, the delegates could propose drastic changes for the Constitution and also try to change the ratification procedure, as the first convention in Philadelphia did in 1787.

Whatever amendments another convention produced, the Congress might claim the right to refuse to submit them to the states. But whatever that outcome, three-fourths of the states must still ratify them to become part of the Constitution, and it is hard to imagine any attempts to avoid that last requirement. This provision, which no one has suggested changing, should assuage any reasonable fears about a wide-open convention, for any amendment that thirty-eight states approved could not be all bad. Nor is ratification likely to be casual for any amendment from now on, after the cautionary tale of the ERA [Equal Rights Amendment].

We should admit that the first Constitution is moribund. Except for a few institutions—the dominant federal structure is not one of them—the original Constitution is largely irrelevant to contemporary public affairs. It set a framework for government on principles widely shared by Americans in the eighteenth century, still held by the majority today, but long abandoned by our governors.

From the Mayflower Compact through the Articles of Confederation, Americans relied upon written fundamental laws to establish, but just as importantly to limit, government. The Constitution was written to correct the inadequacies of the Articles primarily in defense and foreign affairs, for which the new central government was allowed to finance itself. The commerce and currency clauses were intended to *prevent* state regulation and paper money. The Bill of Rights was intended as a further check on the central government, although it has become a license for central control.

Federalism is obliterated now, of course. State and local governments have become franchisees of Washington, dependent upon revenue carrots and submissive to the stick that inevitably followed. There are few domains left now for which federal action is unprecedented. Central government expansion has been driven through every opening in the first Constitution. The antifederalists were right.

The Constitution's careful separation of powers has been wrecked by the growth of Presidential initiative and Congressional delegation to the bureaucracy. The least accountable arms of central government, bureaucracy and the courts, govern most freely. What began as a Constitution of states' and private rights has been turned into a cornucopia of powers.

Building a collectivist state in this century has required demolition of the classical liberal values of the Constitution. Redistribution and regulation have required progressive assaults on property, and an antibourgeois animus has driven the architects of our new constitutional order. The new premises of public policy have turned taxpayers' money into "public funding" or "federal spending." Senator Kennedy has criticized the "blank check for all the spending programs contained in the Internal Revenue Code—the tax expenditure programs." Even the money the government lets you *keep* should not be regarded as "yours," rather as a boon from

Washington. Senator McGovern described Californians voting for Proposition 13 as "degrading hedonists."

Today's rebellion is another middle-class reassertion of the legitimacy of the inherited order, as was the original Revolution. Tax rebels today would agree with the revolutionary aim of John Adams: "I say again that resistance to innovation and the unlimited claims of Parliament, and not any new form of government, was the object of the Revolution."

Most of the values underlying that Revolution and the Constitution were found in the thought of John Locke, who distinguished between occasional violations of natural law inevitable under any form of government and chronic violations constituting a "long train of abuses, prevarications, and artifices" marking degeneration into tyranny, against which rebellion became a right, even a duty. Liberty was conceived as freedom from alien dictation, freedom *from* government, and American conditions seemed so neatly to confirm Locke's views that they became the bedrock of American political thought.

Americans generally expect and accept social change, but primarily outside politics and not as a sweeping purpose of government. They generally support the Lockean emphasis on private property as crucial to individual liberty, and they value achievement still. It is no wonder that mounting redistribution and regulation have evoked today Jefferson's charge against King George III, that "he has erected a multitude of New Offices, and sent hither swarms of Officers to harass our People, and eat out their substance."

Washington is mobilizing to avoid another constitutional convention. The Congress has been alternately soothing the states with promises of a balanced budget by 1981 and threatening them with cuts in revenue sharing. Senator Bayh's Judiciary Subcommittee on the Constitution has been holding hearings on an amendment, and others are on in the House.

President Carter has set up a squad of staff members from the White House and the Office of Management and Budget to pressure governors and legislative leaders in key "battle-front" states not to call for a convention. It is cooperating with a group called Citizens for the Constitution, brought together by Lt. Gov. Thomas P. O'Neill III of Massachusetts to lobby against a convention, backed in turn by labor unions, civil-rights groups, and public-interest groups.

Congress might try to get by with some general resolution for fiscal responsibility, hoping that will stem the tide. Or it might propose a balanced-budget amendment itself, hoping that thirty-eight states will not ratify it after they realize that balancing is not the same as controlling spending. Nearly the most dangerous move, from liberal Democrats' perspective, would be a Congressional amendment to tie annual spending to increases in the GNP. This makes more sense than a balanced-budget requirement and comes closest to satisfying tax rebels.

Democrats in Congress have resisted efforts to set ground rules of a convention by law. Such a law would set the time, place, delegate-selection, and voting procedures and try to set the issue to be considered.

Delegates would probably be elected in House districts, with seats at large from each state. If the thirty-fourth state applied quickly enough and Congress moved soon enough, Washington politicians might prefer delegate selection at the same time as the 1980 elections, so they could get double duty from their campaign funds and organization. That timing would probably help offset the damage to Democrats if the elections of delegates were on a separate ballot, formally nonpartisan, and decided by the issue.

In any case, the advantages of Washington incumbents in such elections would be so great that Congress might be forced to set the size of the convention at, say, twice that of the Electoral College, instead of just one from each district and two from each state. This would still be an assembly of just under 1,100 and would make it easier for Ralph Nader, Cesar Chavez, and William Buckley to join the crowd.

Contemporary liberals warn that reactionaries—meaning

classic liberals who still like the values of the first Constitution—would dominate a new convention. But it is just as likely that leftist groups already strong enough to have entrenched themselves in Washington would be able to take over a convention as well. Unions, especially, as well as the new class of well-educated professional and managerial symbol-specialists who took over the Democratic party in 1972, should do quite well with their organizational and polemical talents. Even if they dominated the convention and enshrined in the Constitution the new politics they have imposed in this century, we would gain a lot just in having the current philosophy of American public affairs set out explicitly. Another convention, with all its possibilities, would force a great shaking-out of American politics. Its drama would cut through the layers of mass apathy and focus popular attention on the fundamental political questions. It would force Americans to consider the kind of people we have become, and the society and government we prefer. It would allow a genuinely New Foundation, if desired.

The proximate issue, controlling government spending, is not some fiscal technicality; it reflects a growing desperation among the governed. The political appeal of the New Deal model—our current constitutional order—has lain in its promise to each voter to take from and control other people for his benefit. But as leveling and legislation have proceeded, a growing majority of Americans have realized that they are now those other people, more often targets of state action than beneficiaries; yet the machinery of regulation and redistribution seems impervious to individual aspiration.

Another convention would force Americans to recall the values of the first Constitution and consider how we have changed as a nation. It would allow a recalculation of the costs of dependence upon government and the benefits of individual responsibility and voluntary public spirit. Another convention could offer perhaps a last chance to make sure we have the government we deserve.

PARTY CRASHERS: A GROWING FORCE IN POLITICS[6]

Newcomers, outsiders and political party crashers are playing a greater role in elections this year [1978] than at any time in the recent past.

Nearly 20 candidates with little political experience won Senate and gubernatorial nominations over favored opponents closely tied to the state or local party apparatus. In most cases these surprise winners ran against the party whose nomination they were seeking. A few, like Wisconsin's Republican gubernatorial candidate, Lee Sherman Dreyfus, did not belong to any party before the thought of seeking office came up.

"I know I crashed the party," Dreyfus told a group of establishment Republicans after he beat their endorsed candidate. "But isn't it more fun and more exciting now?"

Party leaders may not think it is much fun to see their chosen candidates eliminated by neophytes who scoff at the traditional way of doing things. But as parties themselves continue to wither away in many states, and as voters perceive party endorsements as less and less significant, there is likely to be an extended period of party crashing in American politics.

Many of the political elements favorable to outsiders have come together this year. Not since 1970 have candidates been able to spend as much as they want all year on their own campaigns. And as in 1974, when Watergate generated an anti-politician mood, the dominant issue—taxpayer resentment—is well-suited to the outsider's appeal. Perhaps more than in any year, colorful and articulate "outsider" candidates have emerged to run successfully on these issues against

[6] Excerpted from article by Christopher Buchanan, staff writer. *Congressional Quarterly Weekly Report.* 36:3107–9. O. 28, '78. Copyright 1978 Congressional Quarterly Inc. Reprinted by permission.

opponents with extensive party ties but little natural campaign ability.

Why They Win

Money, either from a candidate's pocket or from special interest groups, has always been the single most important explanation for the success of candidates with little party backing or public recognition. The 1970 election, for example, produced several millionaire candidates who dipped into their own fortunes to defeat party favorites. Richard L. Ottinger of New York and Howard M. Metzenbaum of Ohio won surprise victories in Democratic Senate primaries that year, and Milton J. Shapp won the Democratic gubernatorial nomination in Pennsylvania.

One result of the heavy spending in 1970 was the Federal Election Campaign Act of 1971 (PL 92-225) which imposed a $35,000 limit on a Senate candidate's contributions to his own campaign and $25,000 on a House candidate. The 1971 law prevented many Ottingers or Metzenbaums from emerging in 1972 and 1974.

The Supreme Court lifted all personal spending limits on Jan. 30, 1976, in time to affect some congressional primaries but too late for wealthy outsiders to mount the full-year drives for name recognition that such candidates often need.

A few outsiders, such as Rhode Island Cadillac dealer Richard P. Lorber, won late summer Senate primaries, but most of the candidates able to capitalize on the new rules in 1976 were established political figures, such as H. John Heinz III, who spent $2.6 million of his own money to win a Pennsylvania Senate seat.

So the 1978 election is the first one in eight years in which wealthy [and/or famous] outsiders have been able to begin spending money and laying the groundwork months in advance of their primaries. . . .

But more remarkable than . . . "money and fame" stories are the challengers who win without either of these commodities. This year's primaries produced a classic example in Dreyfus, little-known and lightly-regarded chancellor of the University of Wisconsin at Stevens Point, who took the state's GOP gubernatorial nomination from U.S. Rep. Robert W. Kasten Jr., the party choice.

Dreyfus did it largely on personality. Sporting a red vest, looking more like a carnival barker than a candidate or university chancellor, Dreyfus was given little chance of winning the Republican nomination when he joined the party for the first time last December. Kasten had not only the party's endorsement but a highly-touted precinct organization. When asked about his short tenure as a Republican, the glib Dreyfus commented, "My mother always taught me it was polite to join a party before you take it over."

The Right Situation

Dreyfus had more going for him than a red vest and a sense of humor. He had an opponent who played the foil to his criticisms of the Republican Party leadership, big business, and the influence of the city of Milwaukee in state politics.

Most outsiders need not only money, celebrity, and/or personality, but a situation to exploit. When all these things come together, the result is often a victory that nobody predicted, but one that might well have been foreseen. . . .

[Edward J. King's defeat of Massachusetts Governor Michael J. Dukakis in the 1978 Democratic primary] was a victory for a party crasher, and a rebuke to an incumbent who had never cemented his hold on the party establishment. But in order to win, King needed issues. He found a variety of them to use against Dukakis among Massachusetts' working-class Catholic Democrats. He called for an end to abortion, favored capital punishment, and implied that the Dukakis administration had an upper-class liberal tilt. The strategy, one King aide said later, "was to take all the Dukakis haters, put them in a pot, and stir them up to a boil."

King also preached tax limitation and frugal government, much as Maine's James Longley had done among working-class Democrats in winning his state's governorship in 1974.

Like Longley, King could tell voters that as a political novice, he had no part in the taxation and spending policies of the administration in office. . . .

After the Upset

After the outsider wins his primary, he often finds the picture in the general election considerably different. Personal money has less influence, because other sources are willing to get involved. And the image of a candidate running against the system is hard to maintain, particularly if the organization seeks to embrace the outsider in the general election. [Both King and Dreyfus, however, went on to defeat their opponents in their states' general elections in November.—Ed.]

If the outsider is not wealthy, he may need party help, but he risks losing his outside reputation by seeking it.

BIBLIOGRAPHY

An asterisk (*) preceding a reference indicates that the article or part of it has been reprinted in this book.

BOOKS AND PAMPHLETS

Epstein, L. D. Political parties in Western democracies. Praeger. '68.

Fairlie, Henry. The parties: Republicans and Democrats in this century. St. Martin's Press. '78.

Hess, Stephen. America's political dynasties: from Adams to Kennedy. Doubleday. '66.

Hess, Stephen. The presidential campaign. Brookings Institution. '78.

Hess, Stephen and Broder, S. S. The Republican establishment: the present and future of the G.O.P. Harper & Row. '67.

Hinderaker, I. H. Party politics. Holt. '56.

Hoopes, Roy. Primaries and conventions. Franklin Watts. '78.

James, J. L. American political parties in transition. Harper & Row. '74.

King, Anthony, ed. The New American political system. American Enterprise Institute. '78.

Ladd, E. C. Where have all the voters gone? the fracturing of America's political parties. Norton. '78.

Mazmanian, D. A. Third parties in presidential elections. (Studies in presidential selections) Brookings Institution. '74.

Pack, Robert. Jerry Brown, the philosopher prince. Stein & Day. '78.

Rothbard, M. N. For a new liberty; the libertarian manifesto. (Collier Books) MacMillan. '78.

Steinfels, Peter. The neoconservatives: the men who are changing America's politics. Simon & Schuster. '79.
    Excerpt. Esquire. 91:24–30. F. 13, '79. The reasonable right.

PERIODICALS

American Politics Quarterly 7:259–82. Ag. '79. Partisan conversion in the Northeast: an analysis of split ticket voting 1952–1976. C. D. Hadley and S. E. Howell.

American Spectator. 12:5–8. Mr. '79. Picking on Irving. Paul
    Seabury.
°American Spectator. 12:8–10. Mr. '79. Neoconservatism: which
    party's line? Karl O'Lessker.
°Atlantic. 242:52–3+ N. '78. King Midas of "the new right." Nick
    Kotz.
°Atlantic. 244:53–5. S. '79. Referendum fever. André Mayer and
    Michael Wheeler.
Black Enterprise. 9:19. Ag. '78. Blacks and the Grand Old Party.
    Ernest Holsendolph and others.
British Journal of Political Science. 8:129–52. Ap. '78. Partisanship
    reinstated? a comparison of the 1972 and 1976 U.S. presiden-
    tial elections. A. H. Miller
Business Week. p 90+. O. 2, '78. U.S. Labor Party's radical
    crusade.
Change. 10:22–7. S. '78. Proposition 13 and the new conservatism.
    Robert Lekachman.
Commentary. 66:23–9. D. '78. Kennedyism again. Midge Decter.
°Commentary. 67:39–46. F. '79. American politics, then & now. J.
    Q. Wilson.
Commonweal. 106:291–5. My. 25, '79. Why not the best? views of
    Commonweal contributors.
Congressional Digest. 56:67–96. Mr. '77. Federal financing of con-
    gressional election campaigns.
°Congressional Quarterly Weekly Report. 36:3107–9. O. 28, '78.
    Party crashers: a growing force in politics. Christopher
    Buchanan.
°Congressional Quarterly Weekly Report. 36:3110–12. O. 28, '78.
    Third parties are weaker than ever. Rhodes Cook.
Current. 209:17–24. Ja. '79. Future of liberalism; interview of G. S.
    McGovern by Adam Clymer.
Editorial Research Reports. v 2, no 12:703–20. S. 29, '78. New
    right in American politics. W. V. Thomas.
Esquire. 91:36–42. F. 13, '79. The godfather of neoconservatism
    (and his family). Geoffrey Norman.
Fortune. 96:90–5+. S. '77. The unmaking of the Republican Party.
    E. C. Ladd, Jr.
Fortune. 96:212–18+. O. '77. The Democrats have their own two-
    party system. E. C. Ladd, Jr.
Fortune. 96:176–81+. N. '77. Reform is wrecking the U.S. party
    system. E. C. Ladd, Jr.
°Fortune. 99:88–92+. Mr. 26, '79. The new divisions in U.S. poli-
    tics. E. C. Ladd, Jr.

*Harper's. 259:26–8+. S. '79. Rewriting the Constitution. Ben Martin.

Journal of Politics. 39:480–92. My. '77. Presidential voting change in the South: 1956–1972. E. R. Declercq and others.

Journal of Politics. 39:786–93. Ag. '77. On amateur and professional politicians. R. A. Hitlin and J. S. Jackson 3d.

Journal of Politics. 40:708–39. Ag. '78. Political parties and presidential ambition. J. W. Ceaser.

Journal of Politics. 41:680–6. My. '79. Partisan conflict in the Senate and the realignment process. Paul Lechner.

Nation. 226:684–5. Je. 10, '78. Democrats rig the primary rules. Iric Nathanson.

Nation. 227:372–4. O. 14, '78. Conservatism by default. C. B. Gans.

*Nation. 228:360–3. Ap. 7, '79. Socialism comes out: the D.S.O.C.—radicals on a tightrope. Harold Meyerson.

Nation. 229:358. O. 20, '79. Second thoughts [on the Libertarian Party]. Carey McWilliams.

National Review. 30:1002. Ag. 18, '78. New wave; new-style conservatives.

National Review. 30:1531–2+. D. 8, '78. Raising conservative bucks. W. A. Rusher.

National Review. 31:715. Je. 8, '79. Letter from Washington; New right. Cato.

National Review. 31:725–7+. Je. 8, '79. Libertarians & conservatives. Ernest Van Den Haag.

National Review. 31:967–9+. Ag. 3, '79. Has the libertarian movement gone kooky?

National Review 31:1154–5. S. 14, '79. Mid-life crisis; common ground between conservative and liberal Republicans. Alan Crawford.

Nation's Business. 66:13–14. Ap. '78. How real is that trend toward conservatism? J. J. Kilpatrick.

*New Leader. 62:10–11. S. 10, '79. Dreams of a third party. R. J. Margolis.

*New Republic. 180:9–10. Je. 9, '79. Gays in the streets. Paul Robinson.

New York Times. p A 9. Jl. 19, '78. G.O.P. chairman says single issue groups imperil political system. Warren Weaver Jr.

New York Times. p D 10. Je. 4, '79. Eroding party loyalty weakens House leaders. S. V. Roberts.

*New York Times. p A 1+. Je. 18, '79. Activist neighborhood groups are becoming a new political force. John Herbers.

New York Times. p A 27. Je. 22, '79. Mr. Carter's slide rule. William Pfaff.

New York Times. p A 1. Ag. 17, '79. Conservatives plan $700,000 drive to oust 5 Democrats from Senate. Warren Weaver Jr.

New York Times. p LI 20. Ag. 26, '79. Closed primaries: an open question. H. A. Scarrow.

New York Times. p LI 20. Ag. 26, '79. Conservatives capitalize on G.O.P. woes. Frank Lynn.

*New York Times. p B 10. S. 10, '79. Libertarians, foes of big government, nominate Coast lawyer for President. Gladwin Hill.

New York Times. p D 22+. S. 16, '79. Rock stars are into politics again. John Rockwell.

New York Times. p 1+. O. 7, '79. U.S. Labor Party: cult surrounded by controversy. Howard Blum and P. L. Montgomery.

New York Times. p A 31. O. 31, '79. Mr. Carter, 'lobbying' is not a dirty word. M. D. Bromberg.

New York Times. p A 16. N. 1, '79. Thomson joins Presidential race.

New York Times. p A 21. N. 12, '79. Dove + hawk = dawk. Peter Kovler.

New York Times. p B 2. N. 13, '79. Anti-abortion party gaining strength. Frank Lynn.

New York Times. p B 15. N. 13, '79. Helms group helps Conservative cause; club that raised millions to aid senator broadens its scope.

New York Times. p A 31. D. 13, '79. No, let's debate our Iran policy. Arthur Schlesinger Jr.

New York Times. p A 22. D. 13, '79. Crisis in Iran alters '80 race. Adam Clymer.

New York Times. p B 16. D. 18, '79. Dissimilar political activists sue against election campaign law [limiting contributions].

New York Times Magazine. p 158–60+. D. 9, '79. The party's over for the political parties. John Herbers.

*New Yorker. 54:139–40+. My. 8, '78. Affairs of state. R. H. Rovere.

Newsday. p 3. Je. 18, '79. New voters shun party labels.

Newsweek. 92:92. Jl. 24, '78. End of the liberal era. G. F. Will.

Newsweek. 92:13. Ag. 14, '78. New negativism. V. E. Jordan Jr.

Newsweek. 93:104. My. 21, '79. Collapse of certainty. Meg Greenfield.

Newsweek. 93:49–50. Je. 11, '79. Running scared; Senate Democrats. T. Morganthau and others.

Newsweek. 93:96. Je. 18, '79. Pols: the new class. Meg Greenfield.

*Newsweek. 94:31–4+. S. 17, '79. Angry West vs. the rest. Tom Mathews and others.
*Newsweek. 94:44. S. 17, '79. Third parties: politics of hope. Tom Morganthau and others.
*Political Science Quarterly. 92:21–41. Spring '77. The decline of the party in American elections. G. M. Pomper.
  Adapted from The decline of partisan politics, in The impact of the electoral process; ed. by Louis Maisel and Joseph Cooper. (Sage International Election Yearbook, 3) Sage Publications. '77.
Politics Today. 5:12–13. N./D. '78. Public opinion: the new moralism. William Schneider.
*Politics Today. 6:26–28+. Ja./F. '79. Republican Renaissance. Alan Baron.
*Politics Today. 6:58–59. Ja./F. '79. Public opinion: welcome back; with the discovery of two-party politics, the South has finally rejoined the Union. William Schneider.
*Politics Today. 6:36–40. Jl./Ag. '79. Hooray for Hollytics!?! Michele Willens.
Progressive. 42:11. Ja. '78. Building a movement. H. C. Boyte.
Progressive. 43:8. Ap. '79. Stirrings on the left. H. C. Boyte.
Saturday Review. 6:20–3. Mr. 3, '79. Is Congress obsolete?. Tad Szulc.
*Saturday Review. 6:20–3. My. 12, '79. Renegade tax reform: turning Prop 13 on its head. David Osborne.
*Saturday Review. 6:12–15. Je. 9, '79. Power of fetal politics. R. M. Williams.
*Saturday Review. 6:12–14+. N. 24, '79. Power to the people: the crusade for direct democracy. Michael Nelson.
Science. 205:172. Jl. 13, '79. Barry Commoner as first citizen? Constance Holden.
Society. 16:5+. My./Je. '79. Where is the new Jewish conservatism? A. M. Fisher.
Society. 16:5+. My./Je. '79. Liberals, not the Jews, have changed. M. A. Ledeen.
Society. 16:64–9. Jl./Ag. '79. American pastoralism, suburbia, and the commune movement. B. M. Berger.
  Excerpt from On the making of Americans: essays in honor of David Riesman; ed. by H. J. Gans and others. University of Pennsylvania Press. '79.
Time. 109:37. My. 23, '77. New religion for liberals. Hugh Sidey.
*Time. 112:42. N. 20, '78. The decline of the parties. Lance Morrow.
Time. 114:19. Ag. 13, '79. Quixotic quest; Citizens Party.
*Time. 114:20–1. Ag. 20, '79. New right takes aim.
Time. 114:12–16+. S. 10, '79. Hot on the campaign trail.

USA Today. 107:8–9. Ja. '79. Fractured polity in an age of selfishness. R. J. Bresler.

USA Today. 107:2. Ap. '79. Americans distrust their leaders; excerpts from an address. Frank Mankiewicz.

USA Today. 107:17–19. My. '79. Democracy revisited: some American perceptions updated. H. C. Jent.

U.S. News & World Report. 84:24–5. Ja. 23, '78. Why the shift to conservatism; trends in America. G. E. Jones.

°U.S. News & World Report. 85:38–41. S. 18, '78. The two-party system—unique and lasting.

U.S. News & World Report. 85:42–3. S. 18, '78. Ups and downs of political parties.

U.S. News & World Report. 85:30–3. O. 16, '78. In the South, still slim pickings for Republicans.

U.S. News & World Report. 85:34–5. N. 6, '78. Economy and elections: a plus for Democrats; historic trends.

U.S. News & World Report. 86:52–4. F. 26, '79. Conservative cry: our time has come; with interview with R. A. Viguerie.

U.S. News & World Report. 86:62–3. My. 7, '79. Heirs to Dixie barons: new powers in Senate.

U.S. News & World Report. 86:13. Je. 4, '79. New power bloc: urban homosexuals.

°U.S. News & World Report. 87:70–1. O. 15, '79. "Last hurrah" for old-time politics?

U.S. News & World Report. 87:42–3. D. 3, '79. In politics, the media can "make the loser the winner." J. Q. Wilson.

U.S. News & World Report. 87:23–4. D. 17, '79. A nation aroused [by detention of hostages in Iran].

Vital Speeches of the Day. 45:102–7. D. 1, '78. Simple justice and existential victims; Robert Houghwout Jackson Memorial Lecture, October 6, 1978, National College of the State Judiciary, University of Nevada, Reno. W. J. McGill.
    Same. Representative American Speeches: 1978–1979, ed. by W. W. Braden. (Reference Shelf. v 51, no 4) Wilson. '79. p 23–40.

Vital Speeches of the Day. 45:600–4. Jl. 15, '79. The role of the American intellectual community in redefining our national purpose; address, May 2, 1979, Harvard University. P. R. Harris.

°Wall Street Journal. p 30. My. 10, p 20. My. 14, '79. Crisis of the party system, I–II. Arthur Schlesinger Jr.

Washington Post. p A 1+. Ag. 21, '76. Causes vary, demonstrations go on. P. W. Valentine

Washington Post. p A 27. S. 13, '78. The frustrations of single interest politics. D. S. Broder.